ON MY BIRTHDAY
30/30
DEVOTIONAL

Andolelye Parah Wachiye

ON MY BIRTHDAY: 30/30 DEVOTIONAL
Copyright 2020 Andolelye Parah Wachiye

All rights reserved. No part of ON MY BIRTHDAY: 30/30 DEVOTIONAL may be reproduced, stored in a retrieval system, or transmitted, in any form or in any means-by electronic, mechanical, photocopying, recording or otherwise-in any form without written permission; except for the use of brief quotations in a book review or scholarly journal.

Unless otherwise stated, all scriptures are taken from the Amplified Bible (AMP). Copyright 2015 by The Lockman Foundation. Used by permission. All rights reserved.

Produced by Andolelye Parah Wachiye

Printed in the USA

ISBN: 978-1-952426-00-1

Contents

Introduction v
Dedication xiii
Acknowledgment xv

Day 1	I Will Confess My Sins	1
Day 2	I Will Forgive	5
Day 3	I Will Walk with God	7
Day 4	I Will Search Out	11
Day 5	I Will Dwell In the Secret Place	13
Day 6	I Will Seek Peace	21
Day 7	I Will Tame My Tongue	25
Day 8	I Will Enjoy My Spiritual Gifts	31
Day 9	I Will Be Comforted.	35
Day 10	I Will Pursue Favor	41
Day 11	I Will Pray.	47
Day 12	It's My Second Chance	53

On My Birthday ...

Day 13	I Will Be on Guard	59
Day 14	I Will Do The Right Thing	65
Day 15	I Will Seek Counsel	71
Day 16	I Will Give with Understanding	75
Day 17	I Will Be Sensitive	81
Day 18	I Will Be Free	85
Day 19	I Will Take Care of What Remains -1	89
Day 20	I Will Take Care of What Remains -2	93
Day 21	I Will Take Care of What Remains - 3	97
Day 22	I Will Take Care of What Remains - 4	103
Day 23	I Will Take Care of My Physical Body	107
Day 24	I Will Influence	111
Day 25	I Will Ask	117
Day 26	I Will Smile To My Future -1	121
Day 27	I Will Smile At My Future - 2	125
Day 28	I Will Die Daily	129
Day 29	I Will Run and Not Faint	137
Day 30	I Will Be Blessed	141

Introduction

Birthdays are celebrations that remind us of life and the goodness of the life giver—God. These devotionals are a means of establishing the repentant and grateful heart of the one who is celebrated and those around them.

Also, each day stands as a spiritual strategy to help plan and do something different with a goal to bring positives change for the glory of God.

All readers are encouraged to go beyond what each day's devotional suggests. By allowing the Holy Spirit to move in you, you will get clarity for your vision and gain hope for your tomorrow.

Once you see what God sees, and follow what He has declared for you, and add your voice in speaking blessings into your life, you will live to enjoy the blessings of the living God.

On My Birthday …

Life is your one-time gift from God, to be used according to God's plan, not spent toward your self-centered ambitions. Pursue to please God, who has been generous and has extended your life one more year.

Start your walk each day after your birthday by evaluating and asking yourself questions associated to the topic of that day devotion.

- What do I like about my life today?
- What is that I don't like about myself and my circumstances?
- Do I walk in the will of God for my life, or not?
- Am I sure what I'm doing is my perfect vision and purpose from God?
- Do I use the authority and power in my mouth well?
- Do I really know the power in the name and the blood of Jesus Christ?
- Am I grateful? And so on.

Thereafter, ask:

- If I can change that which is not good, will I be willing to participate in bringing the best into my life?

- If I am not sure, where and how can I get the truth?
- If I discover I am not where I need to be, what should be done? And so on.

I encourage you not to be overwhelmed, but rather enlightened. Know that God needs you now more than yesterday or in the days of the past. Allow God to launch you into your assignment at His good and perfect time.

If you know you have wasted many years of doing something you were not commissioned to do by God, accept, repent, and seek God for what is next.

Sitting in guilt and regret doesn't change the past; instead, it ruins your future. Believe the word of God, like that of Galatians 4:4; confess it and speak to that which presents itself as the Goliath, and say, "at the fullness of time, I'm redeemed."

As you read this book, know that it is written and dedicated to a person like you—a person who is alive, and who loves and appreciate life. Not only that, but someone who also wants the future to be better than the past, and is willing to participate in making the change.

These thirty goals are a conversation starter, not to confine you but to free your mind to the even deeper and wider realm of possibilities for better life in God. Dare to explore, improve, and prosper.

You may be wondering what in the world 30/30 means. There may be other meanings of the number 30, but in this case, 30 means perfect timing.

Have you ever wondered why some unpleasant occurrences repeat season after season or year after year? Why others are peaceful, favored, and physically healthy? Why you need to repent, forgive, pray, give, care about others, and guard your heart? And worst of all, why people need to die daily? The 30/30 book has the answer to these questions and more.

Apostle Paul wrote to the Galatians church saying, *"as long as the heir is a child, he does not differ at all from a slave even though he is the [future owner and] master of all [the estate]; ³ So also we [whether Jews or Gentiles], when we were children (spiritually immature), were kept like slaves under the elementary [manmade religious or philosophical] teachings of the world.*

⁴ But when [in God's plan] the proper time had fully come, God sent His Son, born of a woman, born under the [regulations of the] Law, ⁵ so that He might redeem and liberate those who were under the Law, that we [who believe] might be adopted as sons [as God's children with all rights as fully grown members of a family].

⁶ And because you [really] are [His] sons, God has sent the Spirit of His Son into our hearts, crying out, [a]"Abba! Father!" ⁷ Therefore you are no longer a slave (bond-servant), but a son; and if a son, then also an heir through [the gracious act of] God [through Christ]".[1]

This book is intended to change some areas in your life that you are currently not satisfied with to the level of your desired reality. You will be able to change them after you understand your position in God through Jesus Christ (the word).

The Galatian church had experienced freedom and sonship in God, but as they listened and believed false teachers, they lost their inheritance.

Maturity is the key to your progress in God and in your life. The word matures the believer. Knowing and confessing it is the master key to becoming what God through Jesus has promised you. Drifting away from the truth of the word of God is opening the gates to your own prison, and into a life like that of an orphan.

The thirty goals in this book is to position you and allow you to cry (call) Abba-Father in all areas important in a Christian life. In so doing, you will eat the fruits of the power of your tongue[2].

---

1   Gal 4:1, 3-7
2   Prov 18:21

On My Birthday ...

God is waiting and watching upon His word to do what He has send it to do. Words like, "call me while I'm near, seek me while a may be found,"[3] etc.—these promises and all others are a reality in the spiritual realm, waiting for an active child of God to experience them.

You will when you know they have been declared for you, and your spiritual maturity will turn your unhappy life to a fulfilled life in God.

Have confidence in the word of God, for it is eternal and final. No one is able to delay it, change it, or disapprove it. It's not against you—it's for you. The Galatians church didn't know better, and as a result they were deceived. Allow the spirit of the living God to shape your life in alignment with the will and mind of God, day after day, and year after year.

After many years of my life, I have come to realize that I lived the life of servant, instead of that of a child and co-heir with Christ. Year after year, I have faithfully served as a servant and not as daughter.

This was my status for many years until when I was considered spiritually mature— only then did I begin to enjoy serving God from the position of a daughter-father relationship, and oh what a difference! That was when

---

3   Isaiah 55:6-7

King Solomon's words were fulfilled—"there is time for everything under the sun."

I believe, as you read this book, you will be enlightened and shaped to what God's word says you are. Thirty goals in thirty days will help you celebrate your birthday meaningfully and with God in mind. Always remember that God loves you and has extended your life not to survive, but rather to rise higher, and shine brighter.

In this month of your birthday or any time you read this book, imagine how different your life will be after each decree you make. Don't wait on God to do it—He has already declared you blessed. Now it's your turn to activate what lies dormant.

Your unwavering faith, the echo of God's word out of your mouth, and God's timing are keys to unlock the taste, the power, and the divine light for many to follow.

May this be your season to be empowered by the word of God through your own mouth. Verbalize life and address every dry and dead situation and thing in the valley you've ever been in or are in now. Speak as the word of God instructs you—speak not once, but rather speak and continue to speak perfectly, as commanded. Ezekiel didn't speak only once, but he did until those that were not, became[4].

---

4   Ezekiel 37

On My Birthday …

It's your birthday—bless it. Don't curse your life by your silence. As it has been said, planning is one of the keys to success, and not planning is thus one of the keys to a failing lifestyle.

Speaking the word of God in your life is the master key to various and great blessings, and keeping silence is the key to death and life in the midst of dry bones. What would you rather do? Where would you rather be?

> **2 Peter 1:2-3:** *"Grace and peace [that special sense of spiritual well-being] be multiplied to you in the [true, intimate] knowledge of God and of Jesus our Lord. 3 For His divine power has bestowed on us [absolutely] everything necessary for [a dynamic spiritual] life and godliness, through true and personal knowledge of Him who called us by His own glory and excellence".*

Dedication

This book is dedicated to myself, my husband, and our children.

As a family, we are grateful to understand that in God, there is everything we need to live happy and successful lives. What is ours to do is strive to be spiritually mature. We are learning that the spiritual maturity process can be very painful and frustrating, but it must take place.

We embrace the truth that when we come to the end of ourselves and cry Abba Father, He comes to the scene, and what was a challenge to us becomes possible.

We also believe that there is nothing wrong with us possessing riches; what's wrong is when riches possess us. Our perfect timing to speak God's word over us has come and replaced the desire to have material things. What is better than the will and the word of God? The disciples knew this—even when the multitude left, they confessed saying, "We will stay, for Jesus has the word of life."

As a family, we consider ourselves blessed to have decided to dedicate our lives to one another, reminding ourselves of the curse-breaking and life-changing power we possess within us, that is activated through our tongue.

We have refused to keep silent and die, and rather decided to speak life and live.

I also dedicate this book to you, the reader. May God's word in this book change your tomorrow. God blessed and command man to be fruitful, to increase and multiply, and to rule over, subdue, and have dominion over all that is rightly His[5]. This was not only for Adam, but also for all who believe.

---

5   Genesis 1:28

Acknowledgment

Galatians 4:4-7

⁴But when [in God's plan] the proper time had fully come, God sent His Son, born of a woman, born under the [regulations of the] Law, ⁵ so that He might redeem and liberate those who were under the Law, that we [who believe] might be adopted as sons [as God's children with all rights as fully grown members of a family].

⁶ And because you [really] are [His] sons, God has sent the Spirit of His Son into our hearts, crying out, [a]"Abba! Father!"⁷ Therefore you are no longer a slave (bond-servant), but a son; and if a son, then also an heir through [the gracious act of] God [through Christ].

I acknowledge God, my family, my friends, and the body of Jesus Christ. I believe life is successful in its purpose when lived among people and in God, Who is the ultimate source of life and strength.

On My Birthday ...

I thank the Holy Spirit, who helped me to write this devotional. The message of encouragement in each page is to stir up the heart and strengthen the faith of each reader, in order that they seek God and speak as He commands in each day in appreciation of yesterday and anticipation of a better tomorrow.

Thank you my heavenly father, for if it wasn't for your love for the world, it could have been impossible for us to gain the knowledge of your son Jesus Christ our Lord and savior. Your decision to love us while we were yet sinners caused Jesus to take the form of a man and die for us. With His death and resurrection, we are no longer slave to sin, but instead your children and heirs, together with Jesus Christ your son.

On behalf of my family, readers, and the body of Christ, I say thank you.

DAY 1
I Will Confess My Sins

Isaiah 59:1-2

Being privileged to see another year of your life doesn't guarantee wellness. Your wellbeing is in the Lord, as He said,

"Remain in Me, and I [will remain] in you. Just as no branch can bear fruit by itself without remaining in the vine, neither can you [bear fruit, producing evidence of your faith] unless you remain in Me.

5 [a] I am the Vine; you are the branches. The one who remains in Me and I in him bears much fruit, for [otherwise] apart from Me [that is, cut off from vital union with Me] you can do nothing"[6]

You may desire to abide in the Lord for your personal reasons. Whatever reasons you have, small or big, are not

---

6 John 15:4-5

On My Birthday ...

a guarantee to make you walk with the Lord hand in hand. Being mindful of your God-given purpose or assignment will produce a magnetic power/force by which you will be pulled and sustained in the Lord, so that you can make those goals succeed.

I encourage you to get my other book titled, *Humility + Faithfulness = Productivity.* In reading it, you will understand that a purpose-driven lifestyle helps in being productive—a productivity that is not by man's power of ability, but that is from the Lord as a result of abiding in Him.

Another thing that will help you abide in the Lord and be made a winner in all you do or go through is making holiness your priority. Be holy as He is, or else He won't stay or walk with you[7]. I encourage you never to allow sin to become a hindrance to what God has planned for you, this year and beyond[8]. Use the power in your tongue and repent all your sins, and those of others as well.

Make it your top priority to maintain your freedom from the power of sin, with confidence, confessing that you are longer a slave to sin[9].

Instead, make your flesh die daily and with confi-

---

7   I Peter 1:16
8   Isaiah 59:2
9   Romans 6:1-7

dence acknowledge that you will live in the spirt and not in desires of the flesh[10]. If this lifestyle was a priority to Paul and caused him to be who he was and to do what he did for the Kingdom of God despite his many life challenges, we are without excuse.

It's my prayer for you that you take pleasure in living in Christ, for Christ, and with Christ, totally abiding in God so that you can flourish, benefiting yourself, your family, your friends, and the body of Christ.

Make this year a year that you will confess, saying, "This life I live is not I, but Christ living in me"[11]. Follow up with your confessions, and see the word of God being fulfilling in your life. If you don't, ask God why you don't see what His word is saying you ought to see.

Claim the power to increase that is in the word of God. Get rid of all that disrupts the word from growing and bearing much fruit. Be watchful of evil birds, thorns, and rocky grounds, which hinder the power of increase within the seed.

If God commanded the increase, then the seed when sown is expected to bring forth 30%, 60%, and 100%[12].

---

10 1 Corithians 15:31-33
11 Galatians 2:20
12 Matthew 13:8-10

On My Birthday ...

May God heal and bless your place of productivity just because you chose to die to sin and raise up into the Spirit of God.

Most believers find it difficult to be successful, because they neither consult nor acknowledge God in all they do. Choose to turn your heart and repent and invite God in your day-to-day obligation as your resource center[13]. And because God is faithful and watches His word, He will breathe life in you and make you a successful doer of His word[14].

May today be the day that your sins are forgiven, your fear is defeated, your mind is renewed, and your desire to abide in Christ is affirmed.

Because your sins have been wiped away[15], take your position as the light of the world, a house built upon a hill which cannot be hidden[16], and salt to preserve your life and that of others[17]

Always remember, at the fullness of time, you were redeemed[18].

HAPPY BIRTHDAY!

---

13   2 Chronicles 7:14
14   James 1:22-25
15   Isaiah 1:18
16   Matthew 5:14-16
17   Matthew 5:13
18   Galatians 4:4-5

DAY 2
I Will Forgive

Luke 6:37

Most of us wonder why we are constantly sick and surrounded by all kinds of defeat. It's because we are carrying too many baggage of unforgiveness, and we are wearing ourselves out.

I do believe there are many genuine reasons why we get hurt and brokenhearted. I'm also a firm believer that an unforgiving spirit is a killer, utilizing not one weapon, but multiple weapons.

Holding on to unforgiveness is like being in charge of a massive and explosive warehouse, which could blow up at any time, leaving you and other people dead or massively injured. Unforgiveness is not worth the life or destiny of anyone.

There are many books and resources available to help

you learn how you can forgive and enjoy your life free from all toxicity of unforgiveness.

As for me, I encourage you to forgive because God commands us do so. Not to disqualify the validity and importance of all other reasons why we must forgive, but I would rather have you consider the obedience to God first, then walk your way to other reasons. Forgive and you will be forgiven[19].

"Tears shed for self are tears of weakness, but tears shed for others are a sign of strength." -Billy Graham

HAPPY BIRTHDAY!

---

19 Luke 6:37

DAY 3
I Will Walk with God

Jeremiah 33:3

"Call to Me and I will answer you, and tell you [and even show you] great and mighty things, [things which have been confined and hidden], which you do not know and understand and cannot distinguish".

The scriptures are God's breath, packed with His divine life. When He speaks, things become as He desires. Walking with God has many benefits, both spiritual and physical.

My husband has extensively discussed this in his book, titled, *God's Presence: The Hub of Victorious Living*. Get a copy and learn the benefits of walking with God at all times.

God told Jeremiah to call on Him so that He may hear him, and answer him. This tells us that if you are in covenant with God, you need to know the codes that are available through which God's attention is activated.

One of these codes is your voice. Hagar cried, and silence, drought, and emptiness endured; but when the son of covenant Ishmael cried, God answered right away[20]. Not just any voice, but covenant voice will make a difference.

- The voice of love and grace, and not of hatred and human reasoning.
- The voice of humility and generosity, and not pride and self-centeredness.
- The voice of forgiving and groanings, not of revenge.
- The voice of knowledge, understanding, and wisdom, not of confusion and foolishness.

Once God's attention is on you, He has promised that He will tell and show you great and mighty things, even hidden things. Things that the regular mind of a human being is unable to fully understand. All these are yours, but only when you call.

Live a surrendered and covenantal life with God this

---

20 Genesis 21:17

year. Without forgetting to speak, to call, to cry "Abba Father, okay!" When you do, nothing will be impossible, for your God is all-powerful and all-knowing, and will be with you at all times.

Keep your ears, eyes, and heart open, to hear, see, and obey. Make a decision to trust the Lord at all times, and do not rely on your own understanding[21]. You are limited in all ways, but God is powerful and knowledgeable. His ways are higher than yours, and His thoughts are not like yours[22].

Walk with Him no matter what. Start the journey with God in prayer, and study of His word daily[23].

HAPPY BIRTHDAY!

---

21 Proverbs 3:5
22 Isaiah 55:8-9
23 Joshua 1:8

On My Birthday ...

Notes

DAY 4
I Will Search Out

Proverbs 25:2

"It is the glory of God to conceal a matter, But the glory of kings is to search out a matter".

It is not easy for many people to move on, especially when they get their hearts broken. It looks okay or normal to hold on to the past, eve the things that were not good.

Many get stagnated and trapped in the memory of the past, and slow their progress. I do believe it's wise to move on, year after year, entering into a new season with new things to do and enjoy.

We are commanded to pay attention on a new day and not miss what God is doing. This is possible when you choose to do what God requires of you. Your destiny or purpose will not progress if all you bring is the limiting force of the past. All that happens when you look back is that you freeze and die, like Lot's wife[24]. Is that what you want?

> **Isaiah 43:18-19** *states, "Do not remember the former things, Or ponder the things of the past.*[19] *"Listen carefully, I am about to do a new thing, Now it will spring forth; Will you not be aware of it? I will even put a road in the wilderness, Rivers in the desert.*

Searching is not a still or stagnated state, but rather dynamic, with aggressive traits, movement, pursuit, and longing of the heart for something to be found that was lost or something new out of relation of the Holy Spirit.

Make this year a searching year. Because it is written, you will find.

HAPPY BIRTHDAY!

---

[24] **Genesis 19:26**

DAY 5
I Will Dwell In the Secret Place

Psalms 91:1-16

I'm not sure if you know why most soldiers' uniforms, machines, and vehicles have colors and patterns that blend with battlefield environments. It is this way for safety reasons, making it easier for them to hide from their enemies, and hence reduce the risk of being captured or killed.

As soldiers and all in the battlefield obey and follow these guidelines, they are dwelling in the secret place where blindfolding their enemy is possible and profitable.

Great benefits happen when we choose to dwell in the secret place of our God. His strong wings when they hover over us—they are unmovable, our hiding place.

His feathers are thick enough to cover, hide, and

protect us against any extreme. His shadow moves unpredictably, covering us with divine peace and invisibility from our adversary.

The secret place was also used by the Arameans, the enemies of the Israelites. One time, the King of Aram and his officers decided on a good place to camp and use as their hiding place during the fights[25]. Thereafter, God revealed the Arameans plans to the Prophet Elisha, and he went ahead and exposed the plan to his king[26].

This continued for a long time, until the King of Aram got very upset that maybe one of his people was telling their military plans to the enemy. But one officer told the King of Aram that was Elisha, who knew even the King's private discussions in his bedroom, leave alone in their military camps. The exposure caused them to lose the battle time and time again[27].

Elisha was so confident of this secret place in God, where Angels were ordered to protect them wherever they went. These Angels were hidden and operated as secret agents[28]. One day the Arameans' army went for a search for Elisha, and when they find him they were to

---

25 2 Kings 6:8
26 2 Kings 6:9
27 2 Kings 6:10-12
28 2 Kings 6:16-17

arrest him. He was wanted because of what they believed to be causing harm[29]. Their plans failed, were struck with blinded and they got arrested as Israelites captives[30].

When God's presence becomes your secret place, a lot can happen for your favor. And like it was for the Israelites it can happen to your enemies as well. They may plan to arrest you in this area, but God's presence will redirect them to go to another area for their demise.

It's my prayer you make this happen this year. Confuse your enemy until they make fools of themselves and leave you alone. In God's presence, you are invisible and untouchable.

Read **1 Samuel 26:1-11** for a better understanding of my explanations below.

Before David took office as King of Israel, King Saul wanted to kill him so he could keep the office. The enmity between them grow worse, to the point King Saul declared a fight against David. Just like it happened to Elisha and the Aramean army, so it was with David. God always hid David but exposed Saul.

One night, David and his friend Abishai went to the camp where Saul and his army were taking some rest for

---

29 2 Kings 6:13-15
30 2 Kings 6:17-23

the night. For protection, the army surrounded King Saul as he slept. That very night, God wanted to let everyone know that He alone was mighty in battle and faithful in protecting His own; and none could challenge Him.

While God kept David and Abishai hidden, He exposed King Saul, who at the time was an enemy to David. While David and Abishai were walking around and skipping over the sleeping bodies. God was making a statement that nothing can be hidden before Him; He is able to expose and disarm completely.

David, knowing what God could do without his help, didn't raise his hand to any of his enemies. All he did was take Saul's spear and the water jar as proof that David could have killed Saul and his army in their sleep, but chose not do so[31].

They both left the camp, and later on, David started telling him how wrong their pursuit had been[32]. King Saul accepted his wrong and foolish acts against David[33].

What are your battles? Small and silly ones; big and serious ones. List them all, and take them to God in worship, prayer, and praise. Watch Him turn your situation around for the better.

---

31 1 Samuel 26:9-11
32 1 Samuel 26:12-25
33 1 Samuel 26:21

Consider all your enemies God's enemies. You are a successful fighter when you do it in God's presence. Where will you find God's presence? It is in your worship, prayers, praises, and giving, and in His word[34].

Start by making the Holy Spirit your closest partner. He is the only one who knows the mind of God. With God's mind revealed to you in your battles, nothing will catch you off guard. The Holy Spirit is the same who was revealing every secret to Elisha. He will make you outsmart all your enemy's plans and schemes.

Another powerful way of outsmarting the enemy is by praying in the Holy Spirit's language and walking in the gifts of the Holy Spirit, like the word of knowledge, wisdom, prophecy, and discerning of the spirits. These gifts are to reveal and expose gifts, to rout out demons, sickness, infirmities, sin, and hidden binding habits.

Peter and John, under the anointing of discernment and miracle-working power, knew what the man at the gate needed. He didn't need money, but rather healing. And that was what he received, and his life was forever changed.

These gifts are not to embarrass the believer, but rather to embarrass the devil who work behind every

---

34 Psalms 22:3

trial, temptation, illness, addiction, lack, conflict, and sin. These gifts of the Holy Spirit allow the gifted to be above and ahead of the enemy's strategic plans and resist them from happening.

This year, refuse to empower the enemy in any way. He must stay away from your business, so you can keep your position of being above and never beneath; the head and not the tail[35].

The enemy is not supposed to know your God-given secret; but you have the right and ability to know his. Now that you know that secrets are for winners, learn to keep secrets, and win.

Let not every word you receive from God be one for which you have to blow a trumpet for all to know. Knowledge is power. Render the enemy powerless by keeping your mouth shut.

I don't mean that you normally seek the devil and start a conversation with him—no. You may let go of the information in the form of prayer, testimony, or telling your dreams or visions to family or friends, or when the word of prophecy is released.

By God's grace, you are privileged to know God's mysteries and know what he is planning to do. The en-

---

35 Deuteronomy 28:13

emy is limited and must stay that way. No wonder he tries to sneak in one way, but with God's power, he gets exposed and runs away in seven wide ways[36].

Declare war on the spirit that comes to steal your secret information and make it available for the public. Refuse the leak, and bind the spirit that wants you exposed and defeated. Fight in this year, fight in years to come; fight by the blood of the lamb, fight with the sword of the spirit—the word—and fight by the name of Jesus Christ.

We read in Deuteronomy 29:29 that God is selective when it comes to releasing important information. God prefers concealing, and when necessary, He makes it known to His children and His servants. He does so because we are in relationship with Him[37]. If relationship is what determines the exchanging of information, what relationship is there with the devil?

What goes in the family of God need to stays in the family.

HAPPY BIRTHDAY!

---

36 Deuteronomy 28:7

37 John 15:15

On My Birthday ...

Notes

DAY 6

I Will Seek Peace

Hebrews 12:14

God has commanded us to be people who are peace makers. You will be able to receive God's peace if you are willing to share it with others.

People must be ready to make reconciliation between themselves and others and help others to do the same. This mandate is not to be done through our strength, but by grace through the spirit of reconciliation that has been given unto us[38].

With God being our spiritual father, we have some of His traits, including the ability to reconcile. You can access this free ability through prayer. While in prayer, ask for the voice in the blood of Jesus. This voice will speak on your behalf. As Jesus is a peace maker, nothing

---

38   2 Corithians 5:18

else is more important than helping those who call upon His name and activate the power of His blood to speak forgiveness and not revenge.

This will be easy if you consider yourself a sinner desperate to be forgiven. If you don't seek reconciliation with others, how will you convince God to forgive and reconcile with you? Make Hebrews 12:14 your memory verse today. Allow the Holy spirit to help you find methods you can use to seek peace with everyone.

Life is a journey, and most of the times we do wrong, we keep moving on and forget. I encourage you to take time in prayers and allow the Holy Spirit to go through your wrong deeds records and see where you fell short of the ability to pursue peace with others. Once you remember, follow the lead of the Holy Spirit and reconcile with all.

Maybe one of the reasons you are still alive is to reconcile and make peace with those you are not at peace with. King Hezekiah was to die, but before he did, God gave him an opportunity to make things right[39]. God didn't want him to lose anything due to unforgiveness or assumptions.

Often, we assume that we are at peace and getting

---

39 2 Kings 20:1-6

along well with everyone, but sometimes we are not. It's better we ask those around us and pray for the opportunity for reconciliation. Our God is not a respecter of persons[40]. If He did or is doing for one, He will do it for all. The prince of peace was given unto us not only to enjoy eternal peace in heaven; but also to have it while on Earth, enjoying it day after day.

Declare the scriptures, like that in Philippians 4:5-7, saying, *"Let your gentle spirit [your graciousness, unselfishness, mercy, tolerance, and patience] be known to all people. The Lord is near. ⁶ Do not be anxious or worried about anything, but in everything [every circumstance and situation] by prayer and petition with thanksgiving, continue to make your [specific] requests known to God.*

⁷ And the peace of God [that peace which reassures the heart, that peace] which transcends all understanding, [that peace which] stands guard over your hearts and your minds in Christ Jesus [is yours].

The only hope for enduring peace is Jesus Christ.

HAPPY BIRTHDAY!

---

[40] Acts 10:34

On My Birthday ...

Notes

DAY 7
I Will Tame My Tongue

James 3:5-7

I believe you are grateful to be alive today. With that grateful heart, the spirit in you is desiring to do better in important areas of your life. Align yourself with God, so that He may train you in the ways you should go. Proverbs 18:21 reports that the power of life and death is in the tongue. And those who love it will eat the fruits thereof.

That's to say that the tongue is able to make a way for you to walk in. I suggest you tame your tongue so that it can speak better things—the things that have been approved by God.

The tongue is capable of cutting or dividing relationships. Decide to use your tongue to divide and set apart the kingdom of the devil, not yourself, nor the body of Christ. Be whole, be united; refuse to be divided within yourself. Instead, operate from a healthy you.

On My Birthday ...

May your soul, spirit, and body see, desire, and go after what is good for all. Do not allow your mind to think one thing, your mouth to speak another, and your body to go after yet a different thing. That's fragmented life, and in such there is no positive progress.

I believe you desire good things in your life this year. If so, then do yourself a favor—speak cautiously and selectively. Your words will either build or tear down, so choose to build. The all-knowing God has been encouraging us to "be quick to listen and slow to speak"[41]. Why? It's because you don't want to be the enemy of your own life, or of others'.

Ephesians 4:29-30 has more to say about the relationship between our tongues, our hearts, the Holy Spirit, and the people around us.

Do not let <u>unwholesome</u> [foul, profane, <u>worthless</u>, vulgar] words ever come out of your mouth, but only such speech as is good for building up others, according to the need and the occasion, so that it will be a blessing to those who hear [you speak].

30 And <u>do not grieve the Holy Spirit of God</u> [but seek to please Him], by whom you were sealed and marked [branded as God's own] for the day of redemption [the final deliverance from the consequences of sin].

---

[41] James 1:19

31 *Let <u>all bitterness</u> and wrath and anger and clamor [perpetual animosity, resentment, <u>strife</u>, fault-finding] and slander be put away from you, along with every kind of malice [all spitefulness, <u>verbal abuse</u>, malevolence].*

32 *Be kind and helpful to one another, tender-hearted [compassionate, understanding], forgiving one another [readily and freely], just as God in Christ also forgave you.*

All kinds of success is in God; unfortunately, the words out of our mouths offend the very person who is the source of our wellbeing[42]. Speak words that are not offensive to Him, the words that He is longing to see manifested.

Speak life; speak scriptures. Jesus told His disciples that they were clean because of the word He spoke over them[43]. Make those who hear you feel better, clean, healed, and forgiven, and not dirty, guilty, condemned, and abused. Bless and never curse[44].

God loves to speak, He speaks day and night, to the young and old alike. God doesn't take a break from speaking. His Kingdom is strong and prosperous because He made communication a priority.

Not only communicate, but also communicate pow-

---

42 Ephesians 4:30
43 John 15:3
44 Psalms 109:28

erful utterance, with objectives to build His Kingdom and destroy our enemy's altars and camps.

If God speaks all the time, from before time began and on to eternity, then there is also a need for us to speak. If we believe we are in His Kingdom, then we need to learn what is important and what is forbidden.

Speaking is vital, but speaking evil words and worthless talk is forbidden[45]. We must speak answers, not confusion or problems. The answer(s) is in God's word.

Ask God this year for help or training on how to speak, and speak well, delivering sounds and power to change our circumstances and the world. Tongue being a language, it's important to know how to use the language.

In Christian faith or believes, we learn that there are tongues (or languages) of man, of Angels, and of God[46]. If the tongues of men can build and can destroy, I wonder what the tongues of Angels and that of God can do.

They must be powerful—no wonder when God speaks, no one is able to challenge or make it void, but simply to say amen.

It's my desire for believers to be aware that Jesus Christ, the word of God, lives in us[47]. Because He does,

---

[45] Ephesians 4:29
[46] 1 Corithians 13:1; 14:2
[47] Revelation 3:20; Colossians 1:27

may we allow His word, which is life and spirit, to flow out of us as God commands[48].

In this position, we become walking rivers and wells of living water ministering life, saving souls, and making disciples of hope wherever we go[49]. King David said, "Your word is a lamp unto my feet and a light unto my path"[50]. The same is available to you today.

I know you are aware that, if you don't know how to pronounce certain words, there are various pieces of software and online guides available to help with proper pronunciation. Utilizing such free tutorials can help the learner to understand how to use and pronounce any word.

I therefore encourage you to study the scriptures, and as you do, you will learn how to speak like God. Allow the Bible be your trainer, helping you develop in what, when, and how to speak with power, and leading you to experience positive change in your life and the lives of those around you.

Prepare well, so you can eat the (good) fruits of your tongue, this year and beyond. There is power in your tongue—won't you use it?

HAPPY BIRTHDAY!

---

48 John 6:63-70
49 Mark 16:17
50 Psalms 119:105

DAY 8
I Will Enjoy My Spiritual Gifts

I Cor 12 : 4 – 7

As real as your natural birth is, so to is the spiritual birth. Being born of God through the Holy Spirit is divine and real.

Traditionally, parents and guardians long to have their children succeed in their careers and lead their lives happily. So does our spiritual Father. His preparation for successful life is making you His own. You have the abilities to succeed in anything as God Himself does, for you are a spiritually real child of God, with His image and likeness[51].

---

51 John 1:12; Genesis 1:26

On My Birthday ...

This year, pursue that reality of your spiritual lineage with God. Many people do DNA testing just to learn their biological lineage. There is a joy in knowing our ancestral background, including their weakness and also their strength.

I believe there is much to benefit from when a believer makes an effort to know whose they are and go after what their spiritual DNA can offer.

The knowledge of God and His love, existence, power, wisdom, knowledge, creativity, faithfulness, etc. is life empowering and history changing.

Unfortunately, those whom God's existence is for haven't fully believed that God is real and is for them, not to punish them but to make them successful. May you believe, and make God rejoice and sing songs of gladness, for trusting that He is in your midst to save and not to condemn[52].

There is this phrase most of us use as an excuse for lack of commitment: *"easier said than done."* I believe that to make the doing easy like it is in the saying is to rely on the abilities hidden in God and the Holy Spirit.

With Him as a leader, you will be able to draw closer to God and see for yourself the untapped wealth of in-

---

52 Zephaniah 3:16-17

formation, ideas, skills, and courage, and every character within the nine fruits of the Holy Spirt.

I believe once you see, you will partake in what belongs to you and succeed. For without vision, people perish, and the opposite is also true[53]. Allowing the Holy Spirit to partner with you in this life is like entering and dwelling in the realms of all possibilities. For with Him all things are possible, even the ability to know the will and mind of God concerning your life and His purpose on your life[54].

Once you establish trust, faithfulness, and a covenantal relationship with Him, and stay humble, you will have opened a main line into your heavenly Father's thoughts and plans concerning you, which are obviously good and scheduled to happen at the right time[55].

Most of God's children are not successful because they cooperate with God well. They do so not on purpose, but because they lack the skills to manage God's movement and schedule.

Be determined this year that you are not going to miss anything that is scheduled that involves you. You will be able to do that by walking closely with the Holy Spirit.

---

53 Proverbs 29:18
54 Matthew 19:26; Romans 11:33-36
55 Jeremiah 29:11

Don't be silent, either. Walk with Him and engage Him in conversations. Talk to Him as you talk to a real person, for He is also real. He won't judge you for being silly, or too inquisitive—be yourself, ask Him anything, and be the best friend.

It's boring when you have a quiet friend, isn't it? Don't be boring. The spiritual life is real; hence, make real conversations with the Holy Spirit, and succeed.

Don't forget that, the spiritual fruits have a source, i.e. The Holy Spirit.

HAPPY BIRTHDAY!

DAY 9
I Will Be Comforted

Isaiah 40:1

I know of a phrase that the enemy has used to cause many people, even families, to fail. The phrase is, "Divide and rule."

Division is a weapon in the hands of the enemy. God's word encourages unity, oneness, and love, because there is victory and God's blessing when people unite and do things in love and one accord[56].

Depression is the "divide and rule" spirit in disguise. That's why we are encouraged to never leave a depressed person alone. Satan, who comes to steal, kill, and destroy, can use mental disorders like depression to isolate people so he can wear them out and make them prey to destruction. Refuse to be alone. Even in the work of

---

56   Psalms 133:1

God, we are not commissioned to ministry to do it individually, but as a body[57]. Even Jesus sent His disciples two by two[58].

Even the lion, known as the king of the jungle, knows the weakness in division. That's why when he wants to kill and eat, identifies one animal of his choice, and starts pursuing that very one constantly to wear it out and separate it the group of other animals. And in the end, the lion wins.

This year, may you refuse to be destructed, laughed-at, left behind, a target of harm or mockery, lonely, rejected, etc.; instead, speak comfort to yourself and be comforted spiritually and physically.

Don't believe the lie of the enemy that you are the only one who is going through that pain. James 1:2-4 tells the church that various trials and tribulations are common—almost every believer goes through something similar in this journey.

Instead of giving up, we ought to consider it all joy, and beneficial. As we endure, our character also changes to the likeness of that which is expressed in the fruits of the Holy Spirit. Learn more about endurance and other

---

57   1 Corithians 12:12-27
58   Luke 10:1

fruits of the Spirit by reading our other book, titled, *The Fruits of The Holy Spirit: My Identity.*

Therefore brethren, when life issues start challenging you, don't be discouraged—rather, get strong in your faith. Know that you are not the first, and neither will you be last. The path on which you journey is narrow and full of thistles and thorns, not to punish or discourage you, but to lead you to eternal life[59]. Be of good cheer—Jesus overcame, and so will you[60].

Because comfort is yours from the Lord, believe that there's someone who needs to release that to you. This person is that one who 2 Corinthians 1:4 discussed—a believer who has been where you are, endured, and grew in faith, and God came through for them.

Our God is resourceful, and has everything we need now and in the future. He has trained and stationed His obedient and mature people with specific anointings to comfort those in need of His comforting hand. If you are one of them, I encourage you let God know, and He will send the comfort to minister. No need to make the enemy happy by embracing isolation. You are a child of God, who has a loving and large family.

---

59 Matthew 7:14
60 John 16:33

On My Birthday ...

Most of the time, we don't see or receive comfort because we don't comfort others when in need. If you are one of these, learn to comfort God's people. Thereafter you will have planted a seed of comfort to harvest when needed.

It's like the phrase, "What goes around comes around." In our case, this rotating thing is the good. When you receive good, give good; because you have been freely given to, then freely give[61].

Believe in a God of comfort and ask for comfort, and receive it. Jesus needed the comfort, and Angels were sent to minister to Him. He was thus enabled to regain strength for the assignment that was laid ahead of Him[62].

Stay expectant that your Good Samaritan or Angel will be with you at the perfect time. For God doesn't delay or come too early, but always on time[63]. I believe you can ask for someone to pray for you, even those who don't know you.

God has every resource needed for His children, any time and all the time; just ask for it, and you shall receive[64].

---

61 Matthew 10:8
62 Luke 22:42
63 2 Peter 3:9; Isaiah 60:22
64 John 14:14

If all else fails, which it won't, Jesus will comfort you Himself (that's even better). He did this to a woman caught in adultery, to the Samaritan woman at the well, and to the one who had an issue of blood for twelve years.

It's time to be comforted!

HAPPY BIRTHDAY!

On My Birthday ...

Notes

DAY 10
I Will Pursue Favor

Mark 11:14

Being fruitful is not enough, not all you need to succeed. Together with productivity, consumers are vitally needed.

You need believers to enjoy what you are producing. The nine fruits of the Holy Spirit are social-character oriented. You are bearing them to help you get along with other people. Also, these fruits are there to help you do your assignment effectively and efficiently.

Therefore, your day-to-day activities not only benefit you, but also enable you to give service to those around you[65]. You may be anointed, and be very skillful and developed, and still have poor connections with people. Lack of favor blinds consumers from seeing the need to

---

[65] Ephesians 4:11

buy from you or support you in any way. It's like when we say, "Out of sight, out of mind." I believe the sight is the *favor*.

Command peoples' minds to be renewed about you and your services. I believe once people think and put their minds into something, you can consider it done (that's the power of the mind). Declare a thing, and it shall be given you[66].

This negative experience may be due to the absence of favor in your life. Favor will cause people to seek after your talent, or gift, or skill.

Jesus was able to what He did for many reasons. One of them is that He grew up in wisdom, stature, and favor with God and with people[67]. Because of wisdom and favor, Nicodemus went seeking after Jesus in the midnight hour, and he was ministered. Jesus didn't go search for Nikodemus, rather Nikodemus sought after Jesus.

Even if you have a call-in ministry, you don't need to go seeking or begging people to partake of what God has entrusted you with. But you must grow in wisdom, stature, and favor before God and people. Therefore, speak believing that God will draw people you need to minister to you.

---

66   Job 22:28
67   Luke 2:52

One more lesson.

We read in Mark 11:12-25 about the fig tree, which had leaves only and no fruits. One day Jesus was passing by the tree, expecting some figs for him and His disciples, but unfortunately there were none. The figs being a seasonal fruit, we may assume it wasn't the right season. Also, it could have just been a barren tree, without ability to bring forth any fruit at any time.

Regardless, Jesus cursed the tree, saying, "May no one eat fruit from you again"[68]. Now, the curse that was covering this fig tree hindered the growth of favor, and even its original ability to produce.

I do believe that even when the season changed and figs were produced, Jesus commanded no one should ever eat from that tree again. However big, ripe, sweet, etc. the figs were—no one was to eat them.

Imagine that! Favor is much needed. Therefore, plan to pray for favor. May people love you at all times; when you have fruits for them to enjoy and when you have none.

It's my prayer that you grow in favor, and may people be patient and enjoy the time spent together with you. Expect that. In expectation, you must prepare, for expectation demands preparation. If you anticipate to grow in favor with God and with people, then prepare to work.

---

68 Mark 11:14

Whatever you find your hands to do, do it will all your heart and might[69]. Your day-to-day service can stand out if you produce quality goods and services. Be a person of integrity, and loving, hard work[70].

Your God-given gifts/talents are initial or basic abilities that are available to help you execute your purpose. To outshine the rest, you need to invest more on what you were born with. The more you invest in your gift the better the product or services you will bring forth; and that will increase favor before God and people.

God doesn't prosper the sluggards, the lazy and procrastinators. Instead, He commands such to go and learn from the ants[71]. They don't have a leader, but diligently work and keep in stores for future use.

May you this year anticipate, declare, prepare, and increase in wisdom and favor; for the hand of the diligent shall rule and lack nothing[72].

HAPPY BIRTHDAY!

---

69 Ecclesiastes 9:10
70 Ecclesiastes 9:10
71 Proverbs 6:6
72 Proverbs 12:24

Notes

DAY 11
I Will Pray

John 16:24-26

The word *complete* mentioned in the scripture above is defined as the state of being full, intact, total, perfect, whole, or all together; of having all necessary parts, not lacking anything, not being limited in any way, not requiring more work (Jesus's work on the cross is enough), entirely done.

What is it that will make your joy complete?

Many of us think money, material or earthly wealth, makes people fulfilled. It's just a thought, but it's not the truth. Wholesome joy is a result of God's presence in someone's heart. Nothing can replace the joy and satisfaction of being in relationship with the one who is the source of life and existence[73], and the one who shared His likeness and image with us. Not only that, He is the one Whose breath made us living souls.

This knowledge is what our inner beings long to have. And it can be found by anyone who dares to pray, and to pray not for anything but to seek relationship with God.

The disciple needed it, and they asked to be taught how to pray[74]. How bad do you want the *complete joy* in your life? The level of your hunger for the benefits of a lifestyle of prayer will make room for you to pray. Jacob needed to talk to God so bad, and refused to let go of the Angel until he blessed him[75].

Don't wait until something bad happens for you to start praying. Instead, pray at all times, in good and in bad times. If you wait until you have a need or an emergency, you will pray anxiously. In such time, you will be praying to receive things and not for relationship with the God of the things.

Trusting God fully depends on a deeper, firm and developed relationship. This relationship happens when communication is a priority and done daily and frequently.

May God help you this year to pray as a way of com-

---

[73] Acts 17:28
[74] Luke 11:1-13
[75] Genesis 32:22-32

municating with God as your covenant partner. Pray to know God, pray to hear God. Pray as an act of obedience. Don't do it as an obligation, in fear, in confusion, in sin, demanding something, etc. Do it out of love—the love to know God and abide in him. Soon or later, you will be like Enock, who walked with God until he was no more[76].

I believe Enock made his relationship with God a top priority. He took pleasure in having God consume all of his will, desire, and goals, and all that mattered to him was God's will. Just like Paul, he also decided and considered his vision and desires, and the goals of his life dead, but all of Jesus Christ to be alive in and through him[77]. I believe it's our turn to let our self-desires and goals die. This is possible when we decide to dwell instead in the house of prayer.

We read in Luke 2:36-38 about the lifestyle of a widow named Anna, who considered her life of no significance but to pray. She chose to intercede for God's redemptive plan for the world. After the death of her husband, even though it's difficult to be a widow, she could have done something different with her life.

---

[76] Genesis 5:24
[77] Galatians 2:20; Philippians 1:21

Instead, she considered the pleasure of her womanhood and widowhood insignificant compared to that of partnering with God to accomplish what will benefit the world[78].

That decision was making the house of prayer her home, and she prayed day and night till Jesus was presented in the very temple where she was[79].

Are you willing to suffer violence with the Holy Spirit for the salvation of many?[80] Are you willing to let go of the world and its offers and make your body a house of Prayer? Prayers that are directed by the Holy Spirit allow Jesus Christ is form in you.

Your heavenly Father longs for you to occupy the seat next to His son Jesus Christ. It is a place where your flesh desires die and spiritual desires come alive through the Holy Spirit. Such a life is worth all you have, plus life itself.

I believe being an instrument of redemption or a vessel of honor to pray until the world receives its savior is worth the pursuit. May this year be the year you pray a prioritized prayer. For more about prioritized prayers and why and how to pray these types of prayers, read my

---

78 Luke 2:36-38
79 Luke 2:22-38
80 Matthew 11:12; Romans 8:26

other book, *Prioritized Prayers*.

A Biblical hero named Ezekiel's devotional lifestyle carried a miracle, performing anointing and resurrection power. What was considered dead decomposed, wasted away, only a bunch of very dry bones, a witnessing of what had been but was no longer there.

Ezekiel's ability to walk in truth with God, to obey and exchange ideas, brought to life that which was long gone and dead[81]. That anointing can be yours this year.

You may have been in faith and have accomplished some great things for God and your family and even your community. I'm learning that accomplishment can bring an unsettling sense of fear, known as success stress. It's a pressure of its own kind, demanding your attention for another performance, while inquiring about the what, when, where, why, and how of the next goal.

Looking at Elijah, for example as it is written in 1 Kings 18—after a great miracle full of power and fire from God, there came pleasure, demanding him to engage in another contest against Jezebel. This second contest was Jezebel's idea, not God's.

I believe it was wise for Elijah not to participate in it. I recommend what Elijah did—please run and stay away

---

81 Ezekiel 37:1-14

On My Birthday ...

from all of which God is not the author. Do only what He leads you to[82]. If Elijah did, so will you—pray, hear, understand, declare it, and succeed[83].

This year, you may succeed in many areas, and feel the success stress, even then, hiding in God's presence. By way of prayer, you will overcome this and many other stresses of life. For you are called not to be anxious, but to be prayerful[84].

May this year be lifechanging for you in regard to prayer life. May you become bold and enter in the throne room of God, and present others' needs like Queen Ester did[85].

Command your selfishness to depart from you, and passionately walk toward the throne of grace. Know God, and partner with Him to do great things. Believe with me, that there's more to prayer than just praying.

HAPPY BIRTHDAY!

---

82   1 Kings 19:1-21
83   1 Kings 18:30-40
84   Philippians 4:6-7
85   Romans 14:8; Esther 4:16

DAY 12
It's My Second Chance

Eccl 9:11

"I again saw under the sun that the race is not to the swift and the battle is not to the strong, and neither is bread to the wise nor riches to those of intelligence and understanding nor favor to men of ability; but time and chance overtake them all".

I believe you need to have some divine uniqueness in you that will help you to not be left behind when the second chance comes. Referring to Ecclesiastes 9:11 above, I believe that to be in the midst of the swift, strong, wise, intelligent, and skillful demands more than just showing up.

Otherwise, the reality that you are not what they have will overshadow you and leave you feeling like Gehazi, the servant of Elisha. Gehazi became scared for his life, but Elisha knew that they were not alone, but rather with a great heavenly host of Angels who were doing and would continue to do the fighting for them[86].

You need to have the revelation and assurance that God is indeed fighting on your behalf. Your understanding and confidence on this will propel you to a winning row. Without God's presence in your circumstances, there may be many second chances, without you becoming a winner. Maybe you missed the first time, just because you were standing on the position where Gehazi was and not where Elisha was. This time around, switch your position and succeed.

Look at David, in his weakness—unskillful, young, and unappreciated, he was presented before Goliath, who was skillful and experienced, and had armed soldiers. David was placed there not to perish, but to prove before all that there is unseen power in the name of the Lord. This power is active and well able to do anything, ready to fight for whomever believes.

For you to enjoy and be successful in your second chance, you need to be strong in faith, and very courageous, and believe that the giants you see have no spirit to fight you and will witness their downfall[87].

Don't ignore what is in your hands. The power of

---

86 2 Kings 6:15-20
87 Joshua 2:9-11; Psalms 91:8-16

God can flow through anything, especially the weaker things[88]. The power of God performed a lot of miracles as it was hidden in Moses' staff[89]. Also, it was in the little oil in the widow's jar[90]. The same power was within the wordless prayers of Hanna[91]. Most people are not experiencing the power of God in what they have—they forget that God works better with the weak, and affirms the small beginnings[92].

Most of my books and other accomplishments are the product of my littleness, nothingness, and loneliness, of a house mother who didn't want to be one. I now know and believe that there is life-changing power in what seems to be of no use. Time itself, if well used, can bring immeasurable wealth. God can use your availability to do great things, in the spiritual realm and even in the natural. Just tell Him you are willing and available in your second-chance moments.

Don't wait for what is recommended or required in the eyes of people. Remember that in God you live and

---

[88] 1 Corithians 1:27
[89] Exodus: chapters 7-11; 14:21-31
[90] 2 Kings 4:1-7
[91] 1 Samuel 1:15-17
[92] 2 Corithians 12:9-11

have your being[93]. Let Him do what needs to be done in and through you—just believe. If David could have waited to get his uniform, it could have been too late. Maybe he could have never gotten it, for the uniforms were for the experienced and trained solders, which he wasn't.

Even Gedeon could have never fought the Median if he'd waited for his clan to level up, or his family to become in a better position socially and economically; he could have never done it[94]. God had to insist that he was okay the way he was. How so? Because God's power was already available in his weakness.

It's my desire that God reveal to you where His power is for you to use. For some people, it's in their rendering wholehearted services unto God and to others. Peter found it in committing himself to serve God as he fetched people, not fish[95]. Ruth got it in serving Naomi. King Hezekiah promised to serve also.

For some, it's in giving cheerfully[96]. For others of us, it's in obedience to God, to our parents, or spiritual leaders, spouses, business partners, managers at work, the

---

93 Acts 17:28
94 Judges 6:11-23
95 John 21:15-18
96 1 Kings 17:10-17; Luke 6:38

law of the land, etc. Obedience carries powerful anointing—with it, you can move any mountain.

Look at Ruth. Her obedience to the voice of God within her caused her to be included in the lineage of Jesus the messiah. Her second chance came with much responsivities. Her commitment to her mother-in-law, Naomi, and a heart and mind of servanthood fueled her into her second-chance blessings.

May you seek to enter into your second chance, with readiness of heart, mind, and body strength, and with the help of the Holy Spirit, you will seize the moment(s).

HAPPY BIRTHDAY!

On My Birthday ...

Notes

DAY 13
I Will Be on Guard

1Cor 16:13

"*Be on guard; stand firm in your faith [in God, respecting His precepts and keeping your doctrine sound]. Act like [mature] men and be courageous; be strong. ¹⁴ Let everything you do be done in love [motivated and inspired by God's love for us]*".

It's God's will and character to guard and stay on guard. We read this in Psalms 121:4, that the Lord is our keeper—He sleeps not, nor slumbers. He is awake all the time, and His eyes move to and fro, just watching, protecting, caring, taking note, providing, and enjoying what belong to Him, and blessing those who are faithful to Him.

I do believe the Psalmist (King David) sang this psalm from his life experience, and it has been recorded on 1 Samuel 26. One night, when King Saul was in pursuit of him, he learned that only God will never sleep on His responsibility to protect that which He esteems in high regard. As the battle went on, one-night God caused a deep sleep to fall over King Saul and his commanders. Even when David and his armor bearer came, they were unable to wake up and fight. Truly, if God wants to make you a winner, He has so many ways He can do that.

In line with this, David also said that unless the Lord builds the city, they labor in vain, those who build it. David continued to say that if the Lord doesn't guard the city, then the watchmen stand guard in vain[97]. It's our responsibility to take good care of what belongs to us. But doing so relies on our human understanding and abilities, and it may not work effectively. Choose to guard with God.

God desires to be involved in all our endeavors, even the smallest things we do in our day-to-day activities[98]. We are not to plan without saying God's will is to be accomplished first, then ours later[99]. Even when we have done all the labor, we still need to acknowledge that God is our harvesting and resting[100].

What does it mean to be on guard?

---

97 Psalms 127:1
98 Proverbs 3:6
99 James 4:15
100 Luke 12:19

- Be careful to avoid being tricked or getting into a dangerous situation
- Pay attention/take notice
- Be vigilant/cautious/prepared
- Be focused/single-minded
- Be on duty and responsible for guarding a particular place or person
- Be alert and prepared for any attack against you

Take Joseph as an example. He needed to be on guard while at home and away. Unfortunately, he wasn't on guard at home, and that's when trouble got hold of him. I am not suggesting not to trust your own family members, but believe what the Bible says—one's enemies are in his household[101].

Joseph could have learned the first time, when he experienced hostility after he shared his dream with his parents and brothers. I do believe he took the brothers' unhappiness lightly, and hence he wasn't prepared for the attack soon to befall him[102].

But he did good when he was at Potiphar's house.

---

101 Matthew 10:36
102 Genesis 37:18-19

On My Birthday ...

Joseph was careful to avoid being tricked or getting into a dangerous situation, by saying no to what Potiphar's wife demanded. He was aware of his duty and responsibility as a chief in charge of the whole house and the wellbeing of the people in the house. Joseph was vigilant to make sure he didn't go against his master and God, which propelled him far, toward a honorable place in God and before men. Was it easy? No, but staying on guard was the key.

We know that gifts or talents take people before great men, but character keeps them there. One time to be on guard is when your life is flourishing, expanding, and becoming a blessing to many. Success can be very dangerous if not handled well and with God's wisdom.

I do believe your life is better today that it was before, just because you chose to love God and acknowledge Him in all your ways. Because you are better, it's time to be on guard. This will help you flourish, expand and become a blessing to many. When that happens, guard your heart from arrogance, pride, selfishness, laziness, deceit, misleading, etc. by being prayerful and a disciple of Jesus Christ.

Be in good standing with God, and attract people. When they come, you must be standing on solid ground, otherwise you will fall.

Why did Joseph have favor and why was he loved

by leaders of the nation despite his different nationality? Because he made obedience to God a priority.

Genesis 39:2-5: *The LORD was with Joseph, and he [even though a slave] became a successful and prosperous man; and he was in the house of his master, the Egyptian. ³ Now his master saw that the LORD was with him and that the LORD caused all that he did to prosper (succeed) in his hand.*

⁴ So Joseph pleased Potiphar and found favor in his sight and he served him as his personal servant. He made Joseph overseer over his house, and he put all that he owned in Joseph's charge.

⁵ It happened that from the time that he made Joseph overseer in his house and [put him in charge] over all that he owned, that the LORD blessed the Egyptian's house because of Joseph; so the LORD'S blessing was on everything that Potiphar owned, in the house and in the field.

Stay on guard, and make sure those blessings are not making you think anything else other than giving God the glory for what you have and what you have lost[103]. Believe that all are working together for your good, or

---

[103] Deuteronomy 8:10-11

that they will. Stay humble, merciful, and thankful[104].

God's blessings and temptations go hand in hand. Today's victories often lead into tomorrow's trials. Don't give up, but rather commit.

HAPPY BIRTHDAY!

---

104 Mica 6:8

DAY 14
I Will Do The Right Thing

Romans 6:1, 15

We know the phrase, "mistakes are a great teacher." Is this an entry pass to making mistake after mistake? I believe it's not.

As life is a journey, anticipate new experiences. These experiences being new doesn't mean you have to make mistakes to be able to learn from them. The Bible assures us that we are the children of the light, hence no walking in the dark. Also, it's written that he who is born of God overcomes the world[105].

Making plans to do the right thing doesn't mean that you know what the future holds. You are planning to do so because you are aware of who is within you (Christ,

---

105 1 John 5:3-4

On My Birthday ...

the wisdom of God)[106]. Also, it's because God knows everything. Let His eyes lead you in all the right paths[107]. Not only that, but also the scriptures declare that God makes known or advertises the end from the beginning, and from ancient times things not yet done[108].

It's wise to partner with such a powerful God, for nothing will be done or done well without God's enablement. Sometimes, people think that when bad things happen in the process of being obedient, that isa sign that what is being done is not of God. That is not always true.

For example, God commanded the Israelites to leave Egypt, right? Was their leaving easy and with no issues? No. The Egyptian government was not willing to let them go, and they continued to be stubbornly resist their freedom. Ten plagues were not enough to pass a message to let God's people go. When they did, it didn't last—the King commanded the army to pursue them all over again[109]. If you are to judge God's will by the absence of resistance, then you may not do what you need to this year. The enemy will come to bring all kinds of

---

106 Colossians 1:27; 1Corithians 1:24
107 Isaiah 40:13; Job 38:4-7; Psalms 32:8
108 Isaiah 46:9-10
109 Exodus 14:10-31

issues to confuse you, but resist him and he will flee[110]. The enemy doesn't like admitting that he is a loser and failure—that's why he is persistent, but even then, resist him all the more.

Looking back to the Egyptians' and Israelites' fight, we learn that God caused the heart of the Pharaoh to be hardened[111], and determined to pursue them all the way into the red sea[112]. God had it all planned out, even them being swallowed up with the Red Sea and never seen again[113]. Just like the Psalmist sung of in Psalms 91:7-8, God's people are to be protected and their eyes witness are to be witness when the wicked get punished.

That's not enough, but also because you are God's dwelling place, as long as God is in you, you can't help but do the right things. It's not that you are boasting, it's just a fact—how can you do wrong if God is the decision maker and governor of all you do? Brethren, it's time to boast in the Lord, because as He dwells in us and we abide in Him, all we'll become is the people who know their God[114].

---

110 James 4:7
111 Exodus 9:12
112 Exodus 14:9
113 Exodus 14:13
114 Jeremiah 9:24

On My Birthday ...

You may be holding people who need your help about something, just because you don't want to make mistakes. Hesitating, or being unsure, or lacking something, etc. shouldn't keep you stagnant. Ask Gideon—he felt inadequate, was in lack and socially incompetent, but the mighty God in him made it possible[115]. Even after accepting what God wanted him to do, he thought many soldiers on the battle field would give him victory, but he was wrong and insecure[116].

The power that was in Gedeon is in you today[117]. Go ahead and do what you are mandated to do. Don't wait to be skillful, knowledgeable, or socially and economically established. What you must be scared of is relying on your own understanding[118].

Lasting success is in acknowledging God in all you do, for He is the source of all wisdom. The Holy Spirit is in you—allow Him to be your advocate and faithful partner. The Holy Spirit knows the mind of God, and with Him on your team, nothing will go wrong. If it does, God has allowed it, and it is meant to turn around for your benefit and to glorify His name.

---

115 Judges 6:15-16
116 Judges 7:1-7
117 Hebrews 13:8
118 Proverbs 3:5-6

In doing it right, time-keeping skills are mandatory. Mark these three: procrastination, laziness, and forgetfulness. Highlight them as some of the aggressive enemies of your success, of doing things right. Be on time, be on season, and be where God is.

Are you aware of one of the reasons the man at the pool of Bethesda stayed sick for thirty-eight years? It was a timing issue. For the healing to enter his body, two things had to take place simultaneously. First, the Angel with God's healing was to come and stir up the water[119]. Second, this sick person was to be the first person to enter into the pool. Timing skills were a determining factor in the healing of anyone who needed healing around that pool.

They couldn't have received healing if they went in before the Angel, neither if they did after another person went before them. The sick person was to be alert to when the Angels appeared, and despite their illness, they were to be strong and fast enough to enter in quickly, before any other person[120]. This man was unable to take the healing of God in that slow motion; for the things of the Kingdom of God suffer violence, and the violent

---

[119] John 5:1-4
[120] John 5:4

On My Birthday ...

takes them by force. In other words, Kingdom blessings are time sensitive. If you delay, the blessings (offer) become invalid, and you miss the time of your visitation[121].

I believe success in this timing principle lies within the Holy Spirit. Acknowledging Him in all you do, He will help you be skillful in timing, doing it right, and doing it successfully[122].

HAPPY BIRTHDAY!

---

121 Luke 19:44
122 Proverbs 3:5-6

DAY 15
I Will Seek Counsel

Isaiah 11:1-5

I believe you are a spiritual person, and ready to be led by the Holy Spirit in whom all knowledge and wisdom generates[123]. The wise counsel of the Holy Spirit need not necessarily come from Him directly, but can be from any man/woman of God. You will be considered wise and successful when you seek counsel, not once but, as a lifestyle[124].

What I'm going to share below I also taught in chapter ten my other book, *The Pursuit of Freedom*. That chapter gives the reason why we need mentors, leaders, and counselors in our lives. I encourage you to get that book as well.

---

123 Isaiah 11:1-2
124 Proverbs 11:14

On My Birthday ...

Immature people ignore and rebel against the commands of their leaders. Often, they are defiant and are not willing to be under any leader, or seek any advice; instead, they are followers of their own hearts' desires[125].

We encourage you to keep in mind that sometimes, what you think it is the right thing or action may not be[126]. You and I are limited in our ability to see the future, unless God sees through us[127].

The effect of living life in the absence of leaders was disastrous before Christ came and is worse now. We see the consequences of leader-free life in the book of Judges. At such times, people did what they wanted, and it never went well with them[128]. May God help us never to think we own our lives. We are no longer our own. We are God's, and therefore we must learn and accept to be led by God, starting from respecting leadership and agreeing to counsel when appropriate[129]. In desiring to seek counsel, do it with understanding. Match your need and the area(s) of expertise of the counselor. Don't seek

---

125 Proverbs 16:25
126 Proverbs 21:2
127 Psalms 32:8
128 Judges 21:25
129 Proverbs 3:5

addiction counsel from an investor. Know a counselor's areas of practice before you receive their advice.

I encourage you to believe in the advantages of asking and getting advice from experienced people. Not only one—the more, the better[130]. Also, be aware that counsel alone won't give you success. The main work of counsel is to prevent an individual from doing the wrong things, to the wrong people, and at the wrong time—it doesn't do the assignment for you. Therefore, success = counsel + action.

HAPPY BIRTHDAY!

---

130 Proverbs 11:14; 12:15; 15:22

On My Birthday ...

Notes

DAY 16
I Will Give with Understanding

Luke 6:38

It is commanded that we seek wisdom and that all we do must be done with understanding[131], giving included.

I'm learning that there are several types of giving, and each has its own reason why it should be observed. Make this year a year to give with understanding. Understand the types and the reasons why you should give. We see numerous women in the Bible who gave into ministry on different occasions, and they were blessed.

One type I would like to share with you is the giving that is profitable—give where there is an anointing. Knowing that the anointing breaks yokes, give in it and

---

131 Proverbs 4:7

get your freedom[132]. There are different kinds of yokes, like the yokes of sickness, addiction, sin, poverty, lack, relationship and family issues, etc.

Giving to a successful person or ministry is giving into the anointing. The life of a successful person or ministry is a good ground for your seed/gift to grow and bear desired fruits. Why? It is so because in such there is no presence of any hindering spirit, but rather the spirit of blessings.

It is said that people are the product of their environment. That is to say, if you were raised by an alcoholic parent/guardian, you are likely to become an alcoholic at some point in your life. The same happens to those raised in an abusive environment—they can become abusive as well. That's why I would like you to give in a prosperous environment, expecting to acquire such anointing and grace to be successful. This principle is real, and many are not aware of it.

We have heard or said it ourselves that giving to rich people is wasteful. And we get motivated to give to the poor, without knowledge that giving to the poor doesn't break the curse of poverty or any stronghold. It's important to give to the poor—it's God's will for us to re-

---

132 Isaiah 10:27

member the needy. But it's my prayer that we do it with discernment and understanding.

God owns the Earth, and all that is within it, silver and gold, is His[133]. If God is this wealthy, why do we give to Him in the form of offerings and tithes? I believe we do so not to help Him or His kingdom work, but rather we give under His anointing for our good. We give to the wealthy God so we can be partakers of His anointing to prosper. He is the one who gives the strength or grace to make wealth[134].

Studying the parable of a sower will brightly enlighten you on this matter. Finances and wealth belong to God; we are stewards to make more out of what we have been given[135]. In other words, we are like farmers. In Matthew 13, a farmer had an obligation to increase what he had. He had only one method to do that, by sowing.

As the scripture says, he started sowing on the busy footpaths or the streets, next on the shallow and rocky soil, then on the ground full of bushes and thorns, and lastly, he showed on a good fertile or blessed soil. This person was diligent like King Solomon advised[136]; un-

---

133 Haggai 2:8-9
134 Deuteronomy 8:18
135 Matthew 25:14-30
136 Ecclesiastes 9:10

fortunately, his success came from one place only—the rich soil. Mathew 13:9 says that anyone with ears to hear should listen and understand.

All the seed except one was sown in insufficient places, in poor or unfertile environments. Because these places were not ready for the seed, the seed never multiplied. That's what happens if you give to poor or needy people expecting a reward or a harvest; it won't happen. Give to them to help them survive, not for your breakthrough. Be enlightened, and give with understanding- give to those who lack nothing, and become like them.

The wise King Solomon is teaching us the element of faith and diligence as we sow seeds. He says we ought to do it in the morning, and in the evening, and not grow weary[137]. I believe giving is for all, and may we give to the right environments. Give not once but at all times—morning, afternoon, and evenings. We don't know which one will bring forth much harvest[138]. But we don't want to be ignorant, and just scatter them even where the possibility to harvest is narrow or impossible.

Look at the life of the woman who broke her alabaster box[139]. Why did she break it? Why did she have

---

[137] Ecclesiastes 11:6
[138] Ecclesiastes 11:6
[139] Matthew 26:6-13

many oppositions? She broke her treasure box because she wanted to break yokes that were in her life. She was opposed because no breakthrough comes without opposition. Her action wasn't appreciated; instead, she was told she was wasteful. They wanted her to give to the poor, for they thought that would be profitable[140].

The enemy wanted this woman to stay bound and frustrated, by sowing her seed to the needy soil (the poor). So the opposition was coming from the enemy to discourage her form giving into the anointed King, Who had all authority and power to set this woman free, and He did. The same misleading information we have today, that giving to the rich-anointed (Jesus) is wasteful. No wonder many people give to charities and not to anointed ministers or churches. We need to change and renew our minds about giving. We need to give into the Kingdom of God, of which Jesus is the King.

I pray that, this year you get the enablement to discern and act quickly once you know that you are standing on the blessed, anointed, rich soil. Without hesitation, give there. Thereafter, you can bless the needy, for they are always around you[141].

---

140 Matthew 26:9-11
141 Matthew 26:11

On My Birthday ...

Plan to overcome all opposing powers toward your decision on where to plant your seed. May your mind be enlightened, and enabled to give with understanding. Start giving in order to be set free, and gain the grace to prosper.

HAPPY BIRTHDAY!

DAY 17

I Will Be Sensitive

Mark 12:30-31
Matt 22:37, 39-4

Google dictionary defines sensitivity as a state of being quick to detect or respond to slight changes, signals, or influences. Desiring to be sensitive in a positive way means having the ability to notice things quickly, caring about people's feelings, and thinking deeply before you speak. This ability helps the individual to absorb and process, rather than rushing to a decision. Sensitivity grows deeper as the person learns about their needs, and those of others; and it is strengthened by love.

Sensitivity is important for becoming successful in life. It's needed while at home and in public, in one-on-one conversations and in small and large gatherings. Sensitivity is needed at all times, from and for all genders, ages, and cultures. When sensitivity is well practiced, selfishness won't be a prevailing concern.

A sensitive person knows the need for others to be sensitive. With this ability, they are able to pray to God to send more workers to harvest souls for Him. Due to selfishness and self-oriented goals and vision, people's hearts have grown cold, and they are walking far away from the path of servanthood. As a sensitive person, pray, asking God to touch His chosen people to become sensitive to the needs of others and serve them as He will lead.

There is unexplainable peace and joy in meeting other people needs. It's my prayer that you experience that this year. May you experience God's peace, the peace which passes all understanding; may the spiritual eyes of your understanding be enlightened, your mind renewed, and may you stay obedient to the will and mind of God[142]. May you be clothed with the honor and glory of God as a vessel useable at all times[143].

HAPPY BIRTHDAY!

---

142 Philippians 4:7; Ephesians 1:18; Romans 12:2
143 2 Timothy 2:21

Notes

DAY 18
I Will Be Free

John 8:36

John 8:36: *"So if the Son <u>makes</u> you free, then you are unquestionably free" (AMP)*

John 8:36: *"So if the Son <u>sets</u> you free, you are truly free" (NLT)*

What does it take to be free? I believe freedom is possible where there is a savior, faith to be saved, positioning to be saved, and action to make/set free and be freed.

I am learning that there is a difference between **setting free** and **making free.**

In order to set free, freedom must be already in existence. For example, in order to set the book on the book shelf, the shelf must be already there. On the other hand, to make free means freedom wasn't in existence, and has to be newly made.

On My Birthday ...

Looking at the scripture above, the Amplified Bible says *makes*, and the New Living says *set* free. I believe believers need both. We need to be *made* free and *set* free also. In some areas of our lives, we have experienced the redemptive power of God to *make* us new creations in God. And because of trials, tribulations, and difficulties of all kinds causes the faith and obedience to God fade away. At this point we need to be set free from that which holds us captive. Returning home, like prodigal sons and daughters of God.

There are sins that easily entangle the children of God[144]. These sins can cause believers to grow and practice that which is not pleasing unto God. In the constant act of repentance and asking God for help, He is faithful to set them free over and over again. You may fall seven times; God is faithful to restore you[145].

God also is willing to restore some privileges you may have missed in your walk with Him. It's time for evaluation, to see if you have been missing some benefits that were supposed to be yours on a daily basis[146]. Once you notice, list them down and ask God to *set* them back for your usage and success.

---

144 Hebrews 12:1
145 Proverbs 24:16
146 Psalms 68:19

Also, there are those areas where you need freedom for the first time. Do the same—know what they are, list them, and call upon the miracle working name of the Lord to *make* you free from them all. And surely you will, without doubt, be *made* free.

Ask for your safety as well; spiritually and physically. Some accidents are meant to put you in prison as disability. To avoid such, cover yourself with the blood of Jesus to protect you. Knowing that prevention is better than cure, with the blood of the lamb, the Angel of death must pass over, leaving you safe and secure in God[147].

Do not allow the enemy to hold your freedom. Jesus died to make and set you free, physically, mentally, and spiritually. Your freedom and peace that passes understanding is yours to enjoy. Be violent against anything that presents itself to imprison you over what God has declared free. Jesus paid in full the price of your freedom[148]. What remains is the desire, positioning, and action toward that which has been in existence already in Christ Jesus the savior.

HAPPY BIRTHDAY!

---

[147] Exodus 12:23
[148] Galatians 3:13-15; Romans 3:21-31

On My Birthday ...

Notes

DAY 19
I Will Take Care of What Remains -1

Isaiah 43:19

We read in the scriptures that the Earth and all that is within it shall pass away—only God's word lasts forever. We also read that man shall not live by bread (food) alone but by every word that comes from His mouth[149]. What is it that is common in these sentences above? It is the word of the Lord. The word of God is more than instructions, rules, and principles—it's also truth and life[150]. Day after day, things, events, plans, and people pass away, but the word of God remains unaltered[151].

What I would like you to think about today is the

---

149 Deuteronomy 8:3; Matthew 4:4
150 John 6:63
151 Isaiah 40:8; 1Peter 1:25; Matthew 24:35

On My Birthday ...

truth that in God you live and in Him you have your being[152]. You are who you are and where you are not because of your hard work, good planning, connections, academic achievements, talents, family support and history, finances, gender, or age. It's because God has a plan for your life. Because His plan is good, it's important you consider to align with His unfailing thoughts. The thoughts now, for your successful tomorrow[153].

Many people find it easier to look back than not to. Past life experiences, good or bad shouldn't be part of what is happening now. On this day, make conscious effort to focus on what matters for your remaining days of your life. Adjust your priorities on what your mind should be invested in. As we say, tomorrow's success or failure is an outcome of what is being done today, and not what was done in days past.

It's my prayer that this year in your life you chose to partner with God by letting go of all of the past. Good and bad, larger and smaller, significant and insignificant. All are not to be kept in front—they are to be behind you.

We read in Isaiah 43:19 that God is constantly do-

---

152 Acts 17:28
153 Jeremiah 29:11

ing a new thing. If we are not attentive, we may not see, nor partake of the ways and things of God—letting go not only of the events and things, but of people as well. Some relationships are never meant to last your lifetime. Be enabled and know which relationship need to be dissolved and which need to remain. Be very intentional, and ask God for genuine guidance.

When those things, events, and people who are meant to leave your life have done so, then start taking good care of those remaining.

No one remains unaffected after loss. Some broken relationships cause severe damage to the lives of those involved. The pain of damaged relationship(s) is not going to heal if the victims are held hostage at the scene of the event(s). For their safety and restoration, they need to be taken to a safer environment, far from the crime scene. I believe this crime scene is spiritual, and the mind is its field. From the new environment, spiritually, emotionally, financially, materially, and physically, come new activities to build what remains takes place. Unless the shift, the change, the transformation takes place, healing and focus for the future will be hindered.

Start by listing what has remained and be grateful. Your life itself has remained. You are the witness of how many lives you knew and today they are no more. Take

On My Birthday ...

good care of yourself. Sing for joy; allow yourself to say, "Bless the Lord o my soul, and all that is within me, bless His holy name"[154]. In your surrender, the Lord will surely embrace you and partner with you in doing what He has in mind for you.

God never takes away something from your life without replacing it with something better. Enjoy the new; the new that blossoms from the everlasting word of God.

HAPPY BIRTHDAY!

---

154 Psalms 103:1

DAY 20

I Will Take Care of What Remains -2

THE PEOPLE WHO SEND you gifts and greetings and those who came to your party are likely to be good people. With these friends, develop even a deeper relationship, for they are what I call "Remainers." These may be the right people to consider doing meaningful projects together with. Pray about them; be open to the Lord, and when you get an okay to do something, do not hesitate.

Not only people can be "Remainers," but also your body parts or organs. There many ways people lose the functions of certain body parts or organs. Sometimes, not only the functions are lost, but the parts themselves. If this has happened to you in your life, on this day make a conscious decision to appreciate what is still functioning within your body.

On My Birthday ...

Give God your remaining and functioning organs to bless them individually, and cause them to function ever better. God's power shows up in human weakness[155]. Do not sit in the seat of the discouraged and curse God. Rather, praise Him, for there is nothing too complicated before Him. Let not your discomfort cause you to be guilty or hateful, or to complain or curse God. Stay humble, grateful, and trusting that He is aware of your need. Join the Psalmist and worship God in singing the Psalms 84 & Proverbs 18:10.

You may have family members, friends, or neighbors who are struggling due to loss of their body functions and are in need of support to do their day-to-day activity. The support may not necessarily be to enable them to accomplish their daily obligations, but to help them acknowledge God in their difficulties.

Know that life is a precious gift to be enjoyed despite the dysfunctionality of some organs. Research reports that spirituality is a booster to wellness. I know of a man of God for seven years who was under dialysis and was far down the list to receive a kidney donation. Despite many people being on the waiting list, God

---

155 2 Corinthians 12:9

opened a door for him to get the kidneys. This pair of kidneys was not only good and compatible, but also those of a very young person. Because God doesn't pick sides, if He did to this one, He can do it to any who believes and asks Him.

Take care of what remains, not only for that which is yours, but also that which is for others. Choose to be a support system to someone who is grieving the loss of someone, an organ, or the function of the organ. Their difficult situations may be overwhelming, but don't distance yourself. Instead, stay close and be of help; don't walk away, but help them enjoy what has remained in their life.

As you take care of what remains, don't judge, even when you think and feel you should do so. Because sometimes, life gets complicated due to what we allowed in our lives. Like Samson, who lost his power because of exposing what God told him to keep it as a secret[156]. Blaming and pointing fingers could not have helped restore his strength, but taking care of his hair roots did.

Farmers or growers do the same season after season. In expectation of better harvest, the specific plant goes through cutting and pruning of the unwanted branches.

---

156 Judges 16:6-10

On My Birthday ...

Therefore, if the pruning has taken place, rejoice, for the harvest is coming in greater measure and greater value.

HAPPY BIRTHDAY!

DAY 21
I Will Take Care of What Remains - 3

2 Kings 4:2:

"Elisha said to her, "What shall I do for you? Tell me, what do you have [of value] in the house?" She said, "Your maidservant has nothing in the house except a [small] jar of [olive] oil."

Be encouraged; know that it's not over yet. Even when you find yourself like the widow in the Bible, who was surrounded by debtors. She was desperate for a way out and in deep fear for her son's wellbeing[157]. The oil at hand was all she needed to better her life and the life of her son[158].

---
157   2 Kings 4:1-7
158   2 Kings 4:1-7

On My Birthday ...

Make a sound declaration today that you will ask God to reveal to you what remains that is yours to possess. Be ready to hear and accept His report and obey His guidelines. Most believers tend to conform to the ways of this world, thinking and believing that once they gain a certain status socially, financially, or geographically, then they become someone important. This belief is a lie.

It's my desired prayer that each believer comes to an understanding that their value is not because they have anything earthly, but rather is about their spiritual well-being. Making their spiritual status wealthy should be the focus and the day-to-day pursuit.

There is no down payment or initial cost to have this. Its labor free, for it is by grace we have been saved through faith, and not by ourselves, but as the gift of God, not of works[159]. Salvation by faith I believe is a free life transformation from the status of a sinner to that of becoming righteous of God[160].

The truth the believers must know and hold dearly is that the life in us, the breath of God in us, the indwelling of God in us, the presence and covenant of God

---

159 Ephesians 2:8-9
160 2 Corithians 5:21

with us—that is what makes our mortal humanhood extremely valuable. With this divine wealthy status, we can do anything, even changing our lives from the inside out and become focused on the eternal.

Gratefulness is also important to have. The widow never said what she had was not of value, and never desired what other people possessed. Instead, she embraced it and made it work for her good.

It's my prayer that you will not compare yourself with what others think is best—what you have is the best for you. Take good care of it with faith that God will increase it.

Seek God, or God's servants or counsellors or mentors who have a better spiritual understanding of what you are going through. Their advice may reveal the key to your success[161].

Also, study the case of a woman who had the last ounce of flour for dinner and thereafter was expecting to die, as recorded in 1 Kings 17:12-14. After obeying what the man of God Elijah said, she never lacked food. I believe her obedience open a door of increase. Spiritually, she invested, and the increase happened within hours.

May your giving in obedience open great doors to

---

[161] Proverbs 11:14

your nonstop flow of blessings. For the one who gives, it shall be given back to them in a good measure, pressed down, shaken together, and running over[162]. Giving with faith to bear more fruits is taking care of what remains—the seed.

Holy Spirit-led prayers and Godly counsel will help you determine whether what you have is a seed or bread (is it for investment or consumption?). For the woman in 1 Kings 17, she thought what remained was to be consumed. But once she sought and obeyed God's counsel, she knew it wasn't for her to eat but to sow. The result was the enabling of anointing for more and increase, which destroyed the spirit of lack and the pending death[163].

Take time and list all your fear and cares, command the spirit behind each issue to leave you, for you have Christ of your side. He comes so that His body will have life and live more abundantly[164].

In addition, to that, make an effort to know what to do with what is considered little or insignificant. With God, all things are possible, and miracles are still happening. Jesus was able to feed five thousand with little[165],

---

162 Luke 6:38
163 1 Kings 17:12
164 John 10:10
165 Matthew 14:13-21

and He's still the same as He was then, today and forever. The principle is to confess the word of God. Speak His promises back to His throne. Declare promises like, "God will supply all my need according to His riches in glory[166], God will never leave me or forsake me[167], the Lord prepare my table before my enemies[168], let the weak say I am strong, and poor say I'm rich[169], silver and gold belong to my God[170], healing is my daily bread[171]," and more.

I believe when God's word is spoken under the anointing of the Holy Spirit, grace is unleashed, miracles happen, ways are made, and rivers form[172].

Remember, if God is for you, who can be against you?[173]

HAPPY BIRTHDAY!

---

166 Philippians 4:19
167 Deuteronomy 31:6; Hebrews 13:5
168 Psalms 23:5
169 Joel 3:10
170 Haggai 2:8
171 Matthew 15:22-29
172 Isaiah 43:19
173 Romans 8:31

On My Birthday ...

Notes

DAY 22
I Will Take Care of What Remains - 4

Colossians 3:23

Boaz told Ruth, *"I have been made fully aware of everything that you have done for your mother-in-law since the death of your husband, and how you have left your father and mother and the land of your birth, and have come to a people that you did not know before. *[12]* May the* LORD *repay you for your kindness, and may your reward be full from the* LORD*, the God of Israel, under whose wings you have come to take refuge"*[174].

I do consider Ruth and Naomi to be the broken pieces that remained after the family of Elimelech broke apart by death.

Naomi, being the only love that remained in Ruth's

---

174 Ruth 2:8-11

life, chose to take care of her. Her decision was not in vain—she lived to enjoy the blessing pronounced to her by Boaz that she would be rewarded fully. Even before the rewards well fully hers to enjoy, Ruth was willing to keep doing as she had been doing over the years.

Ruth's foreign status, or being a widow, was not what made God's face shine over her; it was her hard work. Ruth had faith in the God of Naomi, and loved, respected, committed to, and served Naomi, the only love that remained in her life.

Ruth never judged Naomi by what she said or what she was going through, but she knew the value was in what remains. Truly, why had all died but Naomi stayed? She knew God had seeing something in Naomi that none of them saw. With that, Ruth refused to let go of that which God was embracing[175].

In John 10:30, Jesus said that His father and He are one. What He sees His father working on, that is what He will do; as it was in Heaven, so it must be on Earth[176]. Why copy God, why follow His desires? It was and should continue to be so, because in Him there is fullness of joy, and knowledge, and in Him all things are possible[177].

---

175 Ruth 1:16
176 John 5:19
177 Matthew 19:26

Why plan to fail, by going after that which God has let go?[178] Rather, go for what God is going after. We know the saying, "It's not over yet, until God says it's over." I encourage you to take good care of what remains, because God is not over with that person, or that thing, or that assignment. If He authored it, then allow Him to finish[179].

The word of God is also the only promise that lasts for eternity[180]. Study God's word, establish yourself in it, and be a doer of all its commands, in obedience to the command to observe it at all times[181]. As long as it is written, it's a firm promise and is fulfilled in Jesus Christ the messiah[182].

Laziness is not God's will. Most people are left with little, because they are lazy[183]. It's God's command for us to have goals for increase and lay down effective plans to increase in all we do. God has invested spiritual and miraculous power to make the increase[184]. It has been declared that all we touch with diligence will certainly

---

178 1 Samuel 16:1
179 Hebrews 12:2
180 1 Peter 1:25
181 James 1:22; Matthew 28:20
182 1 Corithians 1:20.
183 Proverbs 6:11
184 Deuteronomy 8:18

bring forth increase[185]. God watches His word to fulfill it. He commanded us, saying, "Be fruitful, multiply, and fill the earth[186]. Because He spoke it, it must happen—with God all things are possible. You are a wealth carrier. Multiplication abilities are within you; make them manifest this year. Ruth lived to enjoy the results of her faith as she made Naomi's God and people hers by diligent actions. Don't be slothful, but instead obedient to God's leading. Grow in faith that God rewards the diligent[187]. For encouragement, learn from the ants who are without a leader and yet work tirelessly with knowledge and wisdom[188].

HAPPY BIRTHDAY!

---

185 Deuteronomy 28:12
186 Genesis 1:28
187 Hebrews 11:6
188 Proverbs 6:6

DAY 23

I Will Take Care of My Physical Body

1 Cor 6:19

In the above scripture, Apostle Paul is asking us, "Don't we know that our body is a temple of the Holy Spirit?"

Because you are not your own, allow God to do what He desires with your body, including keeping it holy, clean, and protected away from all that are not from Him. Avoid restricting Him and making Him grieved or quenched; rather, let Him be free and happy to live in His own vessel that is made after His image and likeness—You.

Your physical body is what is known as the flesh or physical being. It is the same as what is known to be the enemy of your spirit man[189]. To allow the Holy Spirit to

---

189 Galatians 5:17

be free to move in you is to acknowledge that you understand business. When you pay for services or goods, you are legally allowed to use what you have paid for.

You, being a valuable vessel bought with the price of Jesus's life, and a new creation, born of the Holy Spirit, must be willing to be renewed in your understanding of a new position. A position that was given unto you after you were born again. You must know that you no longer belong to the devil, and neither to yourself. You are God's child[190]. Because you are, don't allow your physical being to live in the old ways and habits. Let the new management take charge of you.

You do that by studying the word of God and living a prayer-full life. Both the word and prayer will enable you to hear God's instructions on how to take good care of what He paid for—You.

We buy what we need, and so does God. God bought you, for He was in love and in need of you[191]. I encourage you to make this year special. Empty the old off your body, and obey the leading of the Holy Spirit on what should be brought in or put on your new and holy body, for God's glory.

---

190 John 1:12
191 John 3:16

What will help you is the understanding of the value of the life of Jesus. If Jesus's life is valuable, so is yours. Jesus gave His own life in exchange for you. You are that precious before Him. If God the father was able to give His only son to have you, what else wouldn't He give to enable you take care of your physical body?[192]

It's a lie from the enemy to have believers eat unhealthy food, not sign up for fitness programs, not buy genuine skin and body care products, with an excuse that these are expensive. Defeat these lies by asking yourself, was Jesus's life not expensive? Was it easy for Him to spend it on you? Jesus's life was not cheap, and your salvation was not an easy take either.

Trust and ask God, who knows your value, for enablement to take care of the quality you. Take good care of your physical body; God wants you healthy. Longevity is not only a prayer away, but also a lifestyle of healthy choices.

HAPPY BIRTHDAY!

---

192 Luke 12:22-32

On My Birthday ...

Notes

DAY 24
I Will Influence

1Kings 3:10-15

John Maxwell believes that anyone who can solve problems will never lack influence.

Look around you. Look at those who are/were celebrating your birthday with you. Look at the gifts they brought to you. Look at the joy and laughter you brought in those who participated in celebrating with you over the years or even this year. Consider that all these happened because someone (hopefully you) is/was influential in the lives of those who have enjoyed your birthday this year.

Most of us don't like questions, and even more so hate to be questioned. I hope you are not of that kind and not scared to answer questions. Because I have one question to ask you. My question is very simple:

- Are you a problem solver?
- Do you find yourself helping most people who seem confused with no idea of what's next?
- Do your personality or acquired skill(s) leave people positively influenced and happy?

As you answer or think for the answer, I would like you to know that life is a journey with many unfamiliar problems. Some people are able to navigate through life's journey easily, but the majority of people are not. Regardless of whether we know what to do or not, life goes on. Hopefully, we meet people who can help us get clarity about what is confusing.

It's my desire that you are or will be one of those people who bring light in dark moments of other people's lives. Not because you have human knowledge and wisdom, but because you have Jesus Christ—the wisdom of God. Pray and trust God that His reconciliatory spirit will be with you as you answer people's questions.

I'm learning that problem solving is a special skill that not everyone has. This skill flows well when a person is in a calm state, mind, and heart, as they draw strength from the ability of God within and relying on truth of the scriptures. For the word of God is divine and inspired of His Spirit with final authority[193]. Therefore, depending on the counsel and final authority of the scriptures is the key to change and success.

The pillar to success in problem-solving and becoming influential is to do it when acknowledging God is a priority, when calm or at peace, when confident, other-oriented, and non-manipulative. Sarah, a wife of Abraham, once was influential and was able to solve a childlessness issue which existed in her home. Unfortunately, the way she did it brought many problems into her life and the lives of those around her. Her approach in many ways was manipulative, and she was anxious, impatient, and intimidated in that she was old and infertile. We influence others to do better when we don't make our issues the priority.

Problem solving demands a wider look at situations before embracing a conclusion. See what life will look like afterwards. Know that some outcomes last a long time, and sometime even for a lifetime. It will be a burden if the solution you offered brought a negative consequence. Be patient; take time to understand the question and involve those whom you think will be impacted by

---

193 2 Timothy 3:15-17

the decision made. When those involved are happy with the perceived or imagined outcome, then conclude.

Life is a precious gift, not to be filled up with unnecessary circumstances that could have been avoided. May this year be your best year of influence. Be confident that you are well able to give the right advice to those who will need it, anytime and anywhere. Just take time to understanding the question, pray about it, know you are not alone, stay calm, and flow.

As much as I desire for you to be a problem solver and a positive influence, I have to tell you that this position is not always going to be a seat of joy. It is so because influential people also have enemies. When God use His people do His will, the enemy attacks them repeatedly. When people's lives are illuminated, saved, healed, restored, knowledgeable, equipped, etc. it pleases God; but the enemy gets angry and start attacking everyone involved. That's when you need to be on guard, and protect yourself through prayer.

Looking at the life of Jesus as a sent one of God to bring answers to all of us, He wasn't accepted by everyone[194]. But those who believed Him were healed, delivered, mended, and raised from dead, and will be with

---

194 John 1:11

Him in eternity[195]. These positive results of His influence were not easily attained. Jesus had to live day by day as a warrior and a fighter. Fighting for His mission, fighting to be an influence and a light in the dark[196]. Apostle Paul also wasn't appreciated by all, and knew what a life he must live. Living a life like that of a sheep waiting to be slaughtered, by God's grace he said, "I die daily"[197].

Refuse to be weakened by the opposing forces that want you to live your life for you. Make known that you are still here for others. With that, you will enter each and every day with the goal to influence someone.

HAPPY BIRTHDAY!

---

195 John 1:12
196 John 8:12
197 1 Corithians 15:31

DAY 25
I Will Ask

James 4:1-3

I'm learning that I don't have to work for or buy everything I need. Some essential things in life I have received for free. James: 4:1-3 encourages getting some of our needs by asking. Make this year different from the past—ask, seek and knock; don't go without just because you don't want to ask[198].

Life is a mystery and a journey in which each individual has first-hand experience. No one is able to relive their days, even though some believe themselves able to do so. Because of new experiences, asking becomes the way to get the information needed or a navigation system to a solution we desperately need.

Unfortunately, the need to ask has been covered with

---

198 Mathew 7:7

stigma. Many people shy away from asking. because asking seems to be a zone of the illiterate and the ignorant. Not only that, it is not freely done because of trust issues. People have been taken advantage of, just because they asked, and more so, asked a wrong person. In such incidents, the one asking gets hurt instead of receiving the genuine answer they needed.

Nevertheless, make this year your asking year. Do so in prayer—ask expecting the genuine answer and not a lie.

Note, in anything, you do it by faith, asking included. For fear of being hurt and judged, many have become dependent on the internet for their inquiry. Before you trust the internet, ask yourself questions like these:

- Who is behind the screen?
- Who is giving these answers?
- How come they seem to know a lot?
- How come the answers are more than what I'm asking?
- Is there anything I don't know about the internet? And so on.

The internet and all the answers it can display have and continue to be developed and engineered by human beings and not God. The same human beings who are capable of hurting you face to face are well able to do so behind the screen. In fact, a human you don't see is more dangerous than the one you do see. Just like it is with people you see—some are genuine and some are not. The same goes for the internet. Not every source of information is trustworthy. Without God, there is no a safe zone.

Internet and computer tricks have been used to lure people with what seems like the answer to their questions. Be very careful—trust God to guide you to the right source and protect you while there. Nevertheless, be determined to ask. Ask from professionals and lay people. Ask the older and the young alike. As long as you are in doubt, ask. In asking, you avoid mistakes, delays, procrastinations, shame, loss, etc. Step on any stigma associated with asking, and believe that as you ask, you are getting wiser and wiser. As you do this by faith in God, God will step in and guide you with His eyes[199]. Approach people with your questions knowing that God is monitoring and leading you to them.

This is your best year—make it so by not taking any rest until you know what you must know. To make your

---

199 Psalms 32:8

plans succeed, ask for help, knowing that without counsel, plans fail, but the more counsel you get, the more your plans will succeed[200]. Always start with God the faithful and wonderful counselor[201]. Then He will lead you to the right counselor each and every time you need one.

Lastly, forget not to help others who need your counsel. Do this by volunteering. Giving your time, knowledge, wisdom, and experience can be directly or indirectly an answer to those you serve. Asking does not necessarily have to be for you; it can be for the other. Start asking. Ask for help. Ask to give help.

HAPPY BIRTHDAY!

---

200 Proverbs 15:22
201 Isaiah 9:6

DAY 26
I Will Smile To My Future -1

Smiling is an action a person must deliberately decide to take. A smile illuminates like light does. Where there is light, there is life. Plants need light to make energy. Looking at influential people like Nightingale, in her Theory, light is one of the five essential elements of healing and wellness. So smiling is essential for turning misery into healing.

Proverbs suggest we smile into our future, that we give light in our tomorrow. No matter how cloudy or stormy, your future may seem to be, keep smiling at it. Speak life as you smile. Kirk Frankly once sang a song, saying, "You look much better when you smile, so smile"

God has granted you another year walk on that favor, with your head up high, without forgetting to smile at every day in your life. The more you do, the firmer the evidence of your sustaining, fighting, and maturing faith will be. And where there is faith, nothing is impossible[202].

- A smile overrides sadness, sorrow, and stress, and relaxes.
- A smile invites, comforts, and assumes safety and acceptance.
- A smile attracts and approves, and is a sign of good news.
- A smile generates positive emotions, and allows your brain to do better.
- A smile suggests a good spirit, and boosts your immune system.
- A smile is medicine. It balances your heart rate, heals pain, and lowers blood pressure.

Some people do not smile not because they have legitimate reason not to smile. It may be that the spirit of shame, envy, ungratefulness, and heaviness is in operation. In such a situation, make a deliberate decision to repent, sing, shout, dance, and in God's presence cast the spirit of heaviness and sadness off your life. Ask God to

---

[202] Mathew 17:20

anoint you with joy, and dress you with the garment of joyful praises[203]. May He fill your mouth with laughter and your lips with shouting[204].

Also, enhance your smile by taking good care or your oral care and hygiene. At all costs, smile at your future, for the Lord will restore you and cause you to laugh, shout, and enjoy His great works in your life[205].

HAPPY BIRTHDAY!

---

203 Isaiah 61:3

204 Job 8:21

205 Psalms 126:1-3

On My Birthday ...

Notes

DAY 27
I Will Smile At My Future - 2

Prov 31:25

Make a list of situations that you believe are like Goliaths, Jezebels, Jericho, mountains, valleys, deserts, and anything that you believe is not your portion and has no right to share your life this year. Take your list into God's presence, and with God's name and authority, go ahead and call them by their names. Enter a war zone with each, canceling their agendas one by one. Make this not a play date; enter into serious, Holy Spirit-taught prayers[206]. Otherwise, it may not work.

Strongholds or desperate enemies are not easy to be moved off where they have made their home. You must have God's strategies with you as you plan and start

---

206 Romans 8:26-27

evicting them. Start by believing that God is your commander in chief, who assumes your battles as His. When you are established in this, consider yourself a winner[207]. Most believers fail, just because they don't know how to allow God to take the lead. This skill is developed after being a spiritual trained soldier in His army.

Take time to learn about God and His ways by studying the scriptures and doing what is written. Also, fellowship with God in Holy Spirit prayers. He will speak into your spirit man. This training is that which Apostle Paul spoke of in 1 Corinthians 14:4, and that of King David in Psalms 144:1, as he prayed, "blessed be the Lord, who teaches my hands to war, and my fingers to fight."

Because God is not a respecter of persons[208], He is willing and able to train you. That's how you allow God to be the man of war and fight on your behalf. With His love, knowledge, and divine interventions, you are more than a conqueror[209]

Be determined this year to learn to pray prayers that are effective—God-trained prayers. As you win your battles, smiling will be evident. Even when you are surrounded by what seems defeat, don't let go of your trust

---

207 2 Chronicles 20:15; Exodus 15:3; Romans 8:31
208 Acts 10:34
209 Romans 8:37

in God. Instead, acknowledge and trust Him even the more. Call Him your Ebenezer and declare His faithfulness of being with you this far[210].

HAPPY BIRTHDAY!

---

210 1 Samuel 7:12

On My Birthday …

Notes

DAY 28
I Will Die Daily

Romans 8:36-37

The life of the flesh is in the blood[211].

Revelation is a powerful and life-changing force.

One morning, I was reading Germaine Copeland's book, the 25th-anniversary commemorative edition of "Prayer that Avails Much," and on page 63 I came across Leviticus 17:11.

After reading it, I was illuminated to see the connection between this scripture and that of Exodus 12:1-7, where the Israelites were told to smear the blood (of the male sheep/lamb or goat, one year old and without defects) on both sides of their door posts. That night, the Lord was to pass through the entirety of Egypt, striking

---

211 Leviticus 17:11

down every first born of both people and animal and bringing judgement to all the gods of Egypt.

Why were they to smear the blood on their doors? It was to serve as a sign, so when the Lord's Angel was passing by to judge over the land, they would be spared.

What they did that night and many other God-commanded events were a shadow to what we are to observe in our new and better covenant. Their obedience spared their lives.

Here is the application:

With the life of the flesh being in the blood, the act of killing the animal was disabling or killing the life of the flesh. The visible blood on the door post was a confirmation that the flesh was dead, and there was no need to kill that which had no life. What does this have to do with us now?

With Jesus being the door leading to spiritual and eternal life, sin and acts of the flesh must be killed. Jesus the holy one knew no sin, but He became sin for us [212]. Like the lamb/sheep or goat without defects, He shed His blood on our behalf. When we enter a safe place of salvation in Him, we are considered holy and righteous unto

---

212 2 Corithians 5:21

God[213]. The power of sin and flesh has been crucified on our behalf. It's no longer us living, but Christ in us[214]. Once you allow judgement to take place by crucifying your flesh, transformation takes place. The old habits will pass away, and behold, the new has come[215].

May you celebrate your birthday knowing that God wants you well and flourish in His Spirit not in your flesh. You are no longer your own; you have been purchased[216].

Like many of us, life has its way to run over and scare us. As you allow the Lord to be all you need, the fear of life-trying moments won't be as impactful as it could have been without His presence. For in God's presence, there is liberty, and no fear[217]. You may not know what tomorrow hold, but God does. Therefore, abiding in Him, all your cares becomes His cares. Know that you are no longer a slave to fear and sin, but free and alive in the spirit[218].

Embrace the unity with fellow believers in the Lord,

---

213 1 Corithians 1:30
214 Galatians 2:20
215 2 Corithians 5:17
216 1 Corithians 6:19-20
217 2 Corithians 3:17
218 Galatians 4:7

and together may the dwelling place of the spirit be larger and stronger. Ephesians 2:20-22 speaks of this spiritual family, saying, *"²⁰having been built on the foundation of the apostles and prophets, with Christ Jesus Himself as the [chief] Cornerstone, ²¹ in whom the whole structure is joined together, and it continues [to increase] growing into a holy temple in the Lord [a sanctuary dedicated, set apart, and sacred to the presence of the Lord]. ²² In Him [and in fellowship with one another] you also are being built together into a dwelling place of God in the Spirit".*

The focus of this day of your new year is to die daily. Why do you have to die daily, when Jesus did on your behalf and His blood is all over the door post?

In such a house as mentioned above, all believers won't enter in God's Kingdom at the same time. Even spiritual growth is different from one believer to another. Because of this, churches are filled with people of different ages and levels of maturity. Don't expect everyone to be mature; instead, understand that deliverance is ongoing. That is to say, Jesus delivered, is delivering, and will deliver those who are His. His words that He is building the church and the gated of hades will not prevail show that He meant business[219].

Looking at salvation, Jesus is doing it in three tenses: past, present, and future. We have been saved[220], are being saved[221], and shall be saved[222]. So as you gather with others this year, don't be easily quenched; rather, be calm, for Jesus is still working on His church. Your part is to crucify your flesh.

I do also believe these three tenses of the salvation process not only speak of people in different level but also speak in terms of redemption of an individual's spirit, soul and body. These three are related to the three stages of salvation known as justification, transformation, and glorification. The past tense is the *justification,* the present continuous tense is the *transformation*, and the future is the *glorification*.

Our spirit man has been delivered, i.e justification, our soul (mind, will, and emotions) is being delivered as an ongoing transformation, and we will be delivered from our flesh when our mortal bodies are given into immortality, i.e being glorified. When Paul said he was dy-

---

219 Matthew 16:15-20
220 2 Timothy 1:9
221 1 Corithians 1:18
222 Romans 5:9-10; 3:13:11

ing daily, he was addressing his soul, which was in need of transformation to the likeness of Jesus. That what we also need to declare is death, day by day.

Speak death to your flesh, willfully say crucify, crucify, and surely you will not see the fruit of the flesh, instead you will see those of the spirit[223].

What do the scriptures mean when they say judgment starts in the house of the Lord? According to 1 Cor 3:16, believers are the house of God, His habitation or dwelling place. Reading 2 Cor 5:21, we learn that the house judgment has already taken place. He who knew no sin became sin and was punished, buried, and resurrected. In all He went through, He was paying the penalty of sins of the house the Lord[224]. This makes me believe that the judgement was done, and now we live not like a slave but as a friend[225].

God loved us so much, and judging His only begotten son on our behalf was His love on display. He knew if He were to be judged, none of us could have survived. Think about this amazing grace this year. Know that Jesus will do anything in His power to have you by His side, now and through eternity.

---

223 Galatians 5.
224 2 Corithians 5:21
225 John 15:15

Desire a deeper relationship with Him, abide in His presence, walk in the spirt with Him, and praise, love, and serve faithfully, this year and always. He deserves your all. No wonder Paul said, "To me to live is Christ and to die is gain"[226]. And David's song says, "All that is within me praise the Lord"[227].

Christ not only died for all; He died for each.

HAPPY BIRTHDAY!

---

[226] Philippians 1:21
[227] Psalms 103:1

On My Birthday ...

Notes

DAY 29

I Will Run and Not Faint

Isaiah 40:31

Knowing God and developing a deeper relationship is the master key to running without growing weary. His presence is the enabling power for the journey or race in this matter. Jesus said abide in me, for away from me you shall do nothing[228].

As you make this statement today, know that it will be easy if God is on your side and is your strength.

Another way to keep running is to know why you have to run. Jesus kept in the race to the end, because He saw the prize ahead: the church, His bride. What are you seeing? Have a vison, then make it bigger. The bigger and more promising it is, the greater motivation you will have.

---

228 John 15:5

Even when your daily goals or plans change negatively or positively, let not your faith and trust in God get affected. May you grow in faith and not decrease or stay stagnated.

Don't forget to call that which is not as it existed; call using God's word[229]. Because of the existing power in your tongue, your confessions have the power to create—life or death[230]. Therefore, confess the word of God and partner with it to create what it has written. That's calling those existing in the spirit to manifest in the natural world for your good. Be determined to stand still, for God will never change His mind about you and your purpose or assignment in life.

Even when you feel insignificant and fearful like Gideon, encourage yourself in the Lord and confess that you are mighty on Earth, and go in that strength[231].

Even if you get concerned and scared like Gehazi, believe greater is He in you than those who are against you[232].

Do all with love, expectations, endurance, and self-control.

---

229 Romans 4:16-22
230 Proverbs 18:21
231 Judges 6:11-23
232 2 Kings 6:17; 1John 4:4

Believe the word of God, as your sword and shield, and gain confidence and fight, knowing that with God you have a winning warrior[233]. For no weapon formed against you shall prosper[234].

May God supply all your spiritual needs so you can be an overcomer. Knowing that weapons of your warfare are not carnal, but mighty in God for the pulling down of all opposing forces and powers and declaring your victory[235].

Run your race; run to win.

HAPPY BIRTHDAY!

---

[233] Psalms 25:3; Romans 10:11
[234] Isaiah 54:17
[235] 2 Corithians 10:4

On My Birthday ...

Notes

DAY 30
I Will Be Blessed

Psalms 68:19-20

19 "Blessed be the Lord, Who daily loads us with benefits, The God of our salvation! Selah. 20 Our God is the God of salvation; And to GOD the Lord belong escapes from death".

Personally, when I hear the word "benefits," I get excited. Because it's a promising word, not of evil but good. It's more exciting to hear from God, who is not a man that He should lie; neither a son of man that He should change His mind[236]. It's assuring to hear such a statement from a God, who is the author of all good and blessed things.

Choose to bless Him this year, even when the reality or circumstances don't look to be beneficial in any

---

236 Numbers 23:19

way. Praise and worship done in the spirit led by the Holy Spirt activate Angelic activities and the presence of God[237]. In such an atmosphere, the Lord becomes your salvation and the maker of a door of escape from the enemy's traps[238].

Believe and bless Him for Who He is—God and master of all, who is able to turn that which the enemy intended to use against you into a foot stool working for your good[239]. Nothing will ever prevent the goodness of God in the lives of God's children.

The problems are always on us. Doubts, fear, pride, sin, and disobedience, just to name a few, open doors to resistance and delays and sometimes failures.

Being celebrated is a powerful weapon against emotional imbalance, rejection, worthlessness, and depression. Where there is joy, there is no sadness.

Therefore, taking time and allowing people to celebrate you on your birthday is the act of faith of blessing your life. It's the opposite of cursing your life. We see what happened when Job was going through pain, sadness, and loneliness. He cursed the day he was born[240].

---

237 Psalms 22:3; John 4:23
238 Psalms 68:20
239 Psalms 21:10-13
240 Job 3:1

As you celebrate your birthday, those in attendance may come with gifts. Receiving gifts is also a blessing. But not all gifts are safe nor are for you. This year, do differently, even when receiving gifts. Pray for all the gifts given to you, cast out evil spirits that may have been attached with the gifts, and break and rebuke any and all negative assignments attached to any given present.

Gifts should be to bless your life and not to curse. The love people have toward you should inspire them to give you good and beneficial gifts. When Jesus was born, He was celebrated and given gifts. His gifts were prophetic and defined His identity and purpose. He received Myrrh, Gold, and Frankincense.

Also, God loved the world and gave His only begotten son as a gift to all who will receive Him[241]. Jesus was a gift not unto pain, bondage, death, or curse, but unto life and living more abundantly[242]. He was the only gift mankind needed to be able to overcome sin and inherit eternal life[243].

In Mathew 7:11, the scripture says that if we can give good gifts to those we care about, how about God? Will He not give the best to those He loves and those who

---

241 John 3:16
242 John 3:15-17
243 Acts 4:12

are willing to ask? That is to say, no one can give better than God.

In this day of being celebrated, ask God for the best He has in store for you. Note, God's gifts are not for selfish gain, but to benefit others. If you think you will have a hard-time-sharing what God gifts you, then let this year be the year to learn to share. Then, next year, ask for spiritual gifts.

It's really difficult having something to benefit the multitude without the ability to do so. It's scary—you will end up putting it aside like the man with one talent did[244]. Being gifted or talented is a sign that you have a purpose in your life, because a gift or talent from God is an enabling tool to do your assignment in Him[245].

May you celebrate you day with gladness that God has got you covered. Embrace and grow in your spiritual gift that God has given you this year. May bearing fruits of the Holy Spirit be your priority. To know more about these fruits and the reasons you need them, get my other book, titled, *The Fruit of The Holy Spirit: My Identity.*

HAPPY BIRTHDAY!

---

244 Matthew 25:14-30
245 1 Corithians 12:7

www.ingramcontent.com/pod-product-compliance
Lightning Source LLC
Chambersburg PA
CBHW031644040426
42453CB00006B/208